The Actor's Menu®

A Character Preparation Handbook

Bill Howey

Compass Publishing • Lakewood • Colorado

The Actor's Menu®
A Character Preparation Handbook
by Bill Howey

Published by
Compass Publishing
P.O. Box 280188
Lakewood, CO 80228-0188

orders@actorsmenu.com

Library of Congress Control Number: 2004106457

ISBN: 09753102-2-4

First Printing

Manufactured in the United States of America

FEB 0 8 2007

I dedicate this book to my son, Chad Howey, who never had a chance to live the menu of his life and to my dad, Jack Howey, who never fulfilled his.

"Bill, I'm in your debt."

–George Clooney

Table of Contents

Acknowledgment

The foremost recognition goes to my wife and business partner, Carla Howey, who helps me realize my dreams. She motivated the writing of this book, was the first to read and offer her ideas as I wrote, and then decided to format and typeset the book herself. A big part of the book is hers.

During the writing of this book I had valuable contributions from many people who offered helpful opinions and noted corrections: Dan Mundell, Robin Freeman, Brian Thompson, and Leslie Thompson.

I had several people who edited/proofread the book at various stages: Donna Beech, Daniel Fusch and especially Nelson Goforth. Nelson also created our website. Kelley Flynn researched the quotes. Bonnie Hofto consulted on cover design.

Thanks to Milton Katselas for the opportunity.

Finally, I want to thank Bret, Tammy and Steve, my children, who remind me of the value of a meaningful menu in life.

Introduction

The Actor's Menu handbook will inspire, ignite or resurrect your acting career, as it does for hundreds of actors who attend my acting workshops. Whether you are new to acting or an experienced actor, this handbook will get you excited.

With The Actor's Menu you will:

+ Examine your current menu of acting choices.

+ Identify undeveloped acting elements that you already possess.

+ Become self-reliant, trusting your talent and your personal choices.

As an acting teacher for more than 20 years, I have watched both new actors and experienced actors make choices from a crudely developed checklist of choices. I liken these itemized selections to a menu, such as you find in a restaurant. Every actor has such a checklist, whether they are aware of it or not. It is formed while we learn, adopting different choices from experiences in acting or in life.

The idea of The Actor's Menu stems from my perception that acting is much like cooking. Cooking is an art, just like music, painting or acting. Each of these art forms combines various elements such as spices, notes, color, and emotions.

Chefs blend culinary ingredients into a concoction to present to the diners. In the same way actors combine character elements to create a character presentation for an audience. Further, in acting, as in cookery, a sixth sense is more essential than keeping to exact proportions.

Your sixth sense enables you to identify acting ingredients that you possess, ingredients that will intensify your acting. As in cooking, selecting ingredients because of an inspiration or impulse is sometimes the most successful way to make an acting choice. In fact, this is often how new items arrive on restaurant menus—as the result of an offhand idea.

Creating a menu whether as an actor or chef, is really a personal journey. Your acting must always be personal as you call upon your deepest feelings, thoughts and ideas. Your personal ideas and impulses will greatly enhance your acting presentations.

Using this handbook, you will learn to see your choices differently. You will discover whether your existing menu choices are workable and which of those ingredients are the most effective. This introspection allows you to see things in a new and different way. I never tell actors what to see. Instead, I coach them to look with new eyes.

With this approach you will restructure your acting syntax. And once your syntax is changed it will not go back to where it was. You will discard the "how do I...?" questions that many actors ask: "How do I become a good actor?" "How do I get emotional?" "How do I be in the moment?"

"How" is the wrong question to ask because any acting question that begins with "how" indicates an actor is not being creative. In my workshops I field such questions with, "You have the answers. Go discover them." To that I often get another question, "How do I discover?" To that there is one answer: Try everything you can think of until the audience is affected, then build your acting menu based on their feedback.

You are not limited in what you can include on your Actor's Menu. Put anything you want on the list and see if that choice affects the audience. In doing so, you will find your own talent and become your own acting coach.

You will test everything and see if it's workable or in need of more development. Once a choice proves captivating, it's added to the menu under an appropriate heading. A restaurant menu lists categories: Seafood, Meat, Pasta. The Actor's Menu has instead: Emotions, Past Experience and Objectives.

Make every section of this handbook an exercise in discovery and passion. Allow each category to challenge you as you create your own dynamic, impassioned and arresting Actor's Menu.

There are six main sections in this book. I call them the Bill of Fare. As in a menu you will begin with:

Starters / Appetizer

Appetizers in a restaurant are designed to stimulate the desire for more. This section will help you reflect on your past experience, reviewing what has or has not worked for you. It will give you a look at what you previously understood, what you thought you understood, and what used to be confusing. You will look over your experiences—successful or unsuccessful. And along the way you might just uncover your own uniqueness.

Entrée - Main Course

Besides being part of a meal, the word *course* also means *unfolding an action*. In the entrée section you start to unfold your foundation for creating your actor's menu.

Essential Ingredients

In this section, various dynamic actions unfold. With the ingredients of Emotion, Objective, Past Experience and Subtext, you will begin to develop a strong character.

Seasonings

You will now flavor your character with your individual choices, using: Improvisation, Masking, Moments and Transitions.

The Actor's Menu Recipe

This section is where you create your character. Time after time I hear how actors walk back to the parking lot after their audition and realize what they should have done or should not have done. This sudden regret is caused by not sticking to a plan, or in this case, a character recipe. In this handbook, you will create many effective recipes comprised of varied ingredients and have the confidence to present them in an audition.

Dessert

Dessert is the sweet at the end of a meal. In this handbook, dessert is when you clear the way to receive an audience's response to your work. It's been said that after the feast comes the reckoning; your reckoning is discovering how you came across. There is nothing sweeter than hearing that your performance was believable and convincing to an audience. From this feedback you will be able to apply it back to those earlier courses, and be the better actor for it.

A note before you begin:

This handbook should be personal to you. The Appetizer section contains questions that you will answer from your own point of view. In order to record these ideas you'll need a journal. This journal will contain your impressions, thoughts and plans. Write down your thoughts as they occur to you. Your journal notes are vital in creating and revising your own personal menu of acting.

Appetizer

Truth in developing your acting skills begins with an honest evaluation of your current thoughts, ideas and beliefs about yourself and your acting. Only you know the real truth. Answer the questions and exercises that appear throughout the book honestly, completely and openly.

You are singular, unique and exceptional because of the individual ideas, thoughts and images you carry in hidden compartments off the unseen passageways of your inner world. These factors become the potent ingredients you will use to create your own, unique Actor's Menu. This uniqueness is what the audience wants to see. Acting has no mysterious ingredients. There is only what each individual brings to his or her acting.

Using your personal acting journal, answer the questions that follow. Your answers will help you begin the process of discovering or affirming your singularity. Your answers, therefore, are for you alone. No one else will see them unless you reveal them, so be honest. Should a more truthful answer occur to you anywhere along the line, go back to the question.

The answers to these questions may very well reveal why your career is lagging, why you can't commit to an acting career or why you can't answer the "how" questions.

Goals

Seneca said: "If you don't know to which port you are sailing, no wind is favorable." Without a specific destination you drift. Set specific, personal goals that motivate you. Actors often believe that their unique ingredients, their qualities determine what goals they can set. In fact, who you are now determines only the point from which you begin your adventure.

Don't compromise your original goal. Nothing is wrong with the goal "to be a movie star," as long as the actions necessary to attain that goal are understood and actively pursued. Actors often set goals and then don't take the necessary steps to make them happen. Results don't happen magically. But there is magic in setting big goals and working to make them happen. The following series of questions is the beginning of accomplishing that magic.

A point of clarification:

Since you should be writing down the answers to all of the questions in the Appetizer and throughout the book, I have labeled each category to make them easier for you to record. For example, the Goal section is identified with a "**G**" and the number of the question.

> G- 1: **What was my original acting goal when I first became an actor?**
>
> G- 2: **What is my current acting goal?**
>
> G- 3: **What is my long-term acting goal?**
>
> G- 4: **What goals have I set and then abandoned?**
>
> > G-4a: **What was my resistance or opposition to those goals?**
>
> G- 5: **What goals do I dare not try to attain?**

These last two questions (G-4 and G-5) are your abandoned goals or goals you dared not try. After review you may find these become your real acting goal.

G- 6: What changes have I made to my acting goals?

Compare your current goal with your original goal (see G-1). Note any difference.

G- 7: What gives me the most excitement from acting?

Reflect on what really moves you, what motivates you.

G- 8: Are my goals devised to fix what I have been told is wrong with my acting?

G-8a: If so, what?

G-8b: Are those goal fixes helping me?

G- 9: Do I think I'm too old to have a goal to be an actor?

If your answer is "yes" consider the following.

The novelist George Eliot (Mary Ann Evans) wrote that age need not be a deterrent to attaining a goal: "You are never too old to be what you might have been."

I stress in my workshops that persistence and self-discovery are the keys to success.

G-10: Have my acting goals changed?

G-10a: If so, why?

G-11: What intermediate steps have I established to attain my goals?

By this point you should either have set a solid goal or revised the goal you previously set. Your goal must excite you and motivate you. Your goal should be personal and specific. It doesn't have to conform to other people's goals, it's yours alone. A personal, exciting goal, one that you love, one that challenges you, will not easily be quashed.

Once you determine your goal, you begin the process of creating the actions you will use to accomplish that goal. Never give up on a goal without testing it and developing it. Test it, re-test it and test it again. As is said: **The third time's the charm**. Never give up on your goal.

What Is Acting?

As an actor you have probably formed an opinion about what acting is.

The next questions relate to your concept of acting. Is it imitation? Mimicry? Transformation? Role-playing? Representation? Reinvention?

Please answer, in your journal, the following question before continuing. Be complete and express your thoughts fully. Even if you find that your answers are confused or not clearly stated, write them down as they occur to you. That confusion may indicate some area you need to explore. It's vital to know your own point of view.

> "A" stands for Acting.

A-1: What is acting to me?

Acting should not imitate or mimic. Acting is not role-playing. The myth about transformation or "becoming" the character seems to come from the audience. When people see a character who is different from what they know about that actor, or a character who strikes them as very real, they naturally consider it a transformation. Actors can hear this feedback and start believing it. But actors can no more transform themselves into another person than they can become a tree. Actors who work or train under this concept are kidding themselves.

Acting is reinvention or representation. An actor reinvents a character by combining the image received from the script with his or her own personal ingredients.

When actors appear to become another person it's a result of an actor's reinvention. An actor wants the audience to believe that what they see is actually occurring.

When you prepare a dish from a recipe, you're not imitating or being, you're recreating the recipe and putting in your own ingredients. You're reinventing that recipe. The same is true when an actor builds a character. Being an actor means bringing yourself to the script.

Good actors are like chameleons who alter their appearance to fit the surroundings while remaining who they are. Chameleons create the illusion that they are the bush, the tree, the limb. It is this ability that is often perceived as transformation.

Acting, then, is really an illusion that creates a subjective response in each member of the audience. An actor isn't really the character; the audience (in the best cases) just believes it.

Acting needs to be approached with the intention to be as real and true to the situation and the character as possible while understanding it is only an illusion.

Actors can only exist as who they are, in spite of any outward show. It is an actor's ideas, thoughts and attitudes that bring a character to life. Now answer these next questions.

A-2: **If I think of acting as representation, mimicry, imitation, becoming or transforming, do I think that because of what I have been told or what I have experienced?**

A-3: **Did I change what I originally believed in order to fit in with others?**

Hidden Acting Agendas

A Hidden Acting Agenda for an actor is a secret belief that exerts control over his or her thoughts and actions. These concealed preconditions cause a lot of trouble for actors when they perform and study acting.

With this section of the handbook, you will begin to learn why Hidden Acting Agendas are so insidious and how to gain control over them. Understanding what and why you have Hidden Acting Agendas will help re-ignite your acting goals.

"HA" stands for Hidden Acting Agenda.

HA- 1: What physical mannerisms do I think are bad in acting?

HA- 2: What attitudes do I think are bad in acting?

HA- 3: What emotions do I think are bad in acting?

HA- 4: What physical mannerisms do I believe are not right for me in my acting?

HA- 5: What attitudes do I believe are not right for me in my acting?

HA- 6: What emotions do I believe are not right for me in my acting?

HA- 7: Is there anything I think I shouldn't do as an actor?

HA- 8: What do I think I can't do?

HA- 9: What do I know about myself and my acting that I believe I need to keep secret?

HA-10: Have I ever really tried to be personal in my acting work?

HA-10a: If yes, what was the result?

HA-11: What embarrassing critiques have I received in the past that I'm still trying to fix when I act?

HA-12: What have I already fixed in my acting because of something I was told was ugly, unattractive or wrong?

HA-12a: What was the fix?

HA-12b: What were the results of that fix?

HA-13: What has someone else told me was "wrong" with my attitude?

HA-13a: How did that affect me?

HA-13b: What was my fix?

HA-14: Is there anyone who told me I couldn't make it, or I didn't have it, that I would really like to prove wrong?

HA-14a: If so, what would it be like to pay them back for their negativity?

Hidden Acting Agendas begin with faultfinding:

"You are too emotional."

"You are too open."

"People who act sexy are degrading themselves."

"Anger shows weakness."

"Your face is off on the right side."

"Your laugh is very inappropriate."

"You never laugh and that means you're too serious."

"Hide your face, if you must cry."

"Everything bothers you."

"Honestly, your hips are big enough for two people."

"You're getting balder."

Beliefs about oneself are formed and then hidden because they point out bad things. Here are some examples of concealed beliefs:

"I must not be emotional."

"I must not be vulnerable."

"Being sexy is wrong."

"Anger shows weakness."

"Only my right side looks good."

"I mustn't laugh too much."

"I must laugh in every scene."

"Crying makes me look ugly and my nose runs."

"I must not be emotionally moved by anything."

"Because my hips are so big, I must sit down as much as possible."

"I must not show the top of my head."

Negative presumptions can be acquired from many sources: friends, family, teachers, directors and even complete strangers. None of them have an impact unless the actor chooses to make them a Hidden Acting Agenda. To make that negative opinion become a Hidden Acting Agenda, the actor has to take it as the gospel truth.

The term for this is *ideé fixe*, an idea that dominates the mind. Hidden Acting Agendas dominate an actor's mind and actions. Let's say someone tells an actor, "You look ugly when you frown." The actor "corrects" the problem of looking ugly by smiling, even when smiling is not appropriate.

These "corrections" become Hidden Acting Agendas motivating an actor to hide the existence of a perceived defect. Actors often take any and all carping to heart and appease the carper by "fixing" the "problem." Too often, these fixed ideas become more important to an actor than the needs of the character and the story.

Don't think there isn't power behind a Hidden Acting Agenda. There is. Students too often tell me, "I'm an open book, ready to absorb your lessons and grow." What they really mean is "I'm ready... as long as you don't make me stand sideways, show my hips, or show the top of my head."

Agendas impede acting progress, almost always preventing an actor from portraying a strong character. Consider that what is "wrong" about you, as dictated by a hidden agenda, may be very "right" for the story and the character.

You may have an obstructing Hidden Acting Agenda if you resist a direction, are unwilling to perform an emotion, attitude or behavior, or if you find yourself compelled to do or not do specific things.

Actors form Hidden Acting Agendas to protect themselves from criticism or ridicule. It's ironic that the very thing an actor is avoiding might generate the quality, attitude or behavior that enlivens the character and story.

Further, the actual source of "You look ugly when you frown" may very well be another person asserting their own hidden agenda, believing they look ugly when they frown. We see in others what we see in ourselves.

There are strong feelings behind a statement such as "anger shows weakness." That statement may come from someone who avoids showing any anger. The intensity of that statement can make the decree so convincing that an actor accepts the judgment. Once a statement like that becomes a Hidden Acting Agenda, it is fixed upon by an actor and prevents his or her character from being dynamic and multi-layered.

Remember, what is "wrong" for you in real life may be "right" for the character on the stage.

Here is an example:

```
                    Character
              I hate you.
```

The actor, adhering to the hidden agenda that enforces "anger shows weakness," shows no emotion or comes up with a mild, muted version of anger. When questioned the actor either protests or mutters something like, "I don't know why I can't get angry," anything to escape the degradation of being weak.

Adhering to a Hidden Acting Agenda denies the character to the audience. Such a Hidden Acting Agenda is one that says, "This is the right way," "Without this you won't make it," or, "Doing that is dangerous." Thoughts like those are not beneficial for any actor.

Now that you have read about these insidious Hidden Acting Agendas, consider the same set of questions again. This time, look for *your* Hidden Acting Agendas.

> **HA- 1: What physical mannerisms do I think are bad in acting?**
>
> **HA- 2: What attitudes do I think are bad in acting?**
>
> **HA- 3: What emotions do I think are bad in acting?**
>
> **HA- 4: What physical mannerisms do I believe are not right for me in my acting?**
>
> **HA- 5: What attitudes do I believe are not right for me in my acting?**
>
> **HA- 6: What emotions do I believe are not right for me in my acting?**

HA- 7: Is there anything I think I shouldn't do as an actor?

HA- 8: What do I think I can't do?

HA- 9: What do I know about myself and my acting that I
believe I need to keep secret?

HA-10: Have I ever really tried to be personal in my acting
work?

HA-10a: If yes, what was the result?

HA-11: What embarrassing critiques have I received in the
past that I'm still trying to fix when I act?

HA-12: What have I already fixed in my acting because
of something I was told was ugly, unattractive or
wrong?

HA-12a: What was the fix?

HA-12b: What were the results of that fix?

HA-13: What has someone else told me was "wrong" with
my attitude?

HA-13a: How did that affect me?

HA-13b: What was my fix?

HA-14: Is there anyone who told me I couldn't make it, or
I didn't have it, that I would really like to prove
wrong?

HA-14a: If so, what would it be like to pay them
back for their negativity?

If the answers to the above questions reveal that, after you
"corrected" the problem, you grew stronger on stage, this would
not be a Hidden Acting Agenda. Instead, this "correction" would
be a valuable ingredient to be added to your menu.

Payback

Vindication or payback is one class of Hidden Acting Agenda that doesn't hinder, but intensifies an actor's intention to succeed. Proving someone wrong for their negativity can cause unbelievable pleasure. Payback may not be "the right motivation," but it works. And because it is not "right," it's hidden. Payback is viable as long as it only causes harm to the "rightness" of the faultfinder.

Protest, however, can also become the motivation to vindicate oneself. This objection can excite you to become so effective that the faultfinder has his or her negative feedback thrown back in their face.

The desire for payback may be the only thing that moves you to action. It can cause you to overcome any obstacle that stands in your way of reaching that moment when you confront whoever told you "you can't" or "you don't have it" and present the evidence, proving him or her wrong.

The positive action of seeking vindication, rather than keeping the churning resentment inside, is to direct that potentially self-destructive energy into actions that "show them how wrong they were."

Excellence Is A Habit

Aristotle said: "We are what we repeatedly do. Excellence, therefore, is not an act but a habit." If you repeat your actions that stem from Hidden Acting Agendas, they will become a habit, a bad habit. Excellence in acting is being who you are, free of Hidden Acting Agendas.

When receiving a critique from an acting teacher or director that is hard to hear, actors either reject or accept the criticism. The rejection is often the result of a Hidden Acting Agenda. On the other hand, acceptance without any thought or consideration is passive. It is best to accept with the intention to review and represent the choice in order to create the most powerful effect on the audience. This is aggressive. Good actors are aggressive.

Your Acting History

"If you would understand anything, observe its beginning and its development."

–Aristotle

Your acting history is vital to the understanding of who you are and what you can offer as an actor. Avoiding your acting history can impede your progress. If you do not know your history you are doomed to repeat its weaker moments.

With these questions, honestly view your acting history.

"H" stands for history.

> **H-1: Why did I start acting?**
>
> **H-2: What stories do I like to tell?**
>
> **H-3: What stories do I like to see?**
>
> **H-4: What stories do I like to experience?**
>
> **H-5: What have I been told about my ideas?**
>> **H-5a: Did that criticism change my ideas?**

Take another look at whether you have ever been disrespected because of your ideas.

H-6: What, if anything, did I change as a result of what I was told about my ideas.

H-6a: Is that change a Hidden Acting Agenda?

H-7: What acting training have I had?

H-7a: With whom?

H-8: What have I been told about my acting?

H-9: Did I change anything in my acting as a result of what I was told?

H-9a: If so, what?

Rejection can either be used as the reason to quit or as the motivation to fire yourself up with the desire to prove that person wrong. There is nothing bad about finding motivation from the intention to pay someone back. It may in fact be a lot healthier than succumbing.

H-10: Has anyone told me that I can't act?

H-10a: Am I using that as motivation or as a reason to quit?

H-10b: If so, is it helping?

H-10c: If not, should I let that negative motivate me?

If you like the idea of payback, imagine there's someone who would gladly tell you that you "can't." Imagine this person deserves to be paid back for that. This imagination might be all you need to galvanize all your desires and actions.

Coming Across
Or How Others See Me

People style their hair, wear makeup or dress in designer threads to create a positive, desirable image that will affect other people. Most people care how they come across to others.

As an actor, you should be completely invested in how you come across to others, both as yourself and as your characters. How you come across means you are either understandable and convincing to an audience or not. The action of a character must align with what an audience knows and believes.

A common fault of actors is not knowing one piece of vital information: how they come across. Rather, actors focus on how they feel about how they came across.

After a scene in my workshop, actors hear about how they came across, not a myriad of opinions about what they should have done. This forces the actors to develop and test their own ideas.

Actors must develop an ability to receive feedback about how they come across. They must also learn to translate directorial opinions or comments into how they came across. That way actors can maintain what is true for them.

What is true for you is usually hard won. Original ideas are often laughed at initially, if not completely rejected. But, with persistence, these ideas become applauded. Pessimistic individuals may start out ridiculing your idea but as you persist those same people will change and accept your new ideas. Always persist with the ideas you believe in.

Actors celebrate when a casting person tells them, "You were great. Just right on. Thank you for coming in," or "Loved what you did." Hold the champagne until you see a contract or hear, "You've got the part." Many people feel it's necessary to say nice things to actors who are believed to fall apart if they are told the truth after an audition. It's also easier to tell actors what they want to hear than deal with the attitudes and emotions resulting from telling them the truth.

If you come across as funny, people will laugh. If you come across angry, people will back up. If you come across sad, people will be sympathetic. If you impress casting people, they will eventually cast you.

One place to get an idea of how you come across is a good acting workshop. Another place to really find out is at auditions. If you come across convincingly, you have a good chance of callbacks, if not landing the role. There is one fact: if you are convincing and continue to be convincing, audition after audition, you will eventually be cast.

There is one undeniable truth concerning how you come across in auditions and that is: If you got a callback or got the part, you came across well.

"CA" stands for Coming Across

CA-1: **How do I think I come across in auditions?**

CA-2: **How do I think I come across in class?**

CA-3: **How do I think I come across in comedy?**

CA-4: **How do I think I come across in drama?**

CA-5: **How do I think I come across on camera?**

CA-6: **How do I think I come across overall?**

If you answer, "I don't know" to any of these questions, you need to find out.

Using Feelings Vs. Feedback

Using your "feelings" to judge how you come across is very risky. These feelings are usually expressed: "I have a feeling he doesn't like me" or "I have a feeling I did a bad job." Neither feeling has any proof to back it up.

These feelings are different from emotional responses. These self-created suspicions can be the source of your decision to change some aspect of your acting, including quitting altogether. Feelings stimulated by cause—a hurt animal, a touching greeting card or an affecting script—are natural and necessary to an actor. But feelings that originate from false assumptions—such as, "because he looked at me weird, I feel that he doesn't like me" or "because she smiled, she likes me"—can be harmful.

The harm comes from basing decisions on those false self-generated beliefs without actual proof. A casting agent may say, "Thank you, good job," and without knowing for sure, you leave the audition deciding that is the way to audition every time. Or you vow never to audition that way again because of a negative feeling you got when all the agent had was a really bad headache.

How you feel about how you come across can be the result of many things—hunger, a Hidden Acting Agenda or even a fight with a significant other.

A feeling can be stated as a perception, such as, "I have a feeling it's going to rain." But don't confuse a perception with a misconstrued idea, such as telling yourself, "I have a feeling I'm not doing well." Develop the ability to distinguish the difference. This helps prevent negative attitudes.

Find out whether you make decisions about how you come across based on feedback you get from others or if you rely on feelings. If you are unsure about how you come across, it might be because of a Hidden Acting Agenda. Hidden Acting Agendas are created when you think you may have come across inappropriately.

There are working actors with unique quirks. I'm sure these actors knew they came across as quirky, but they didn't let that deter them. They did the work convincingly; in spite of the fact their eccentricity may have bothered other people.

Knowing how you come across after using any and every idea, impulse or hunch you have, will give you a menu of delectable choices.

In the following questions, give not only an answer to the question, but also insert the name of everyone who has had an impact on you because of an adverse or positive comment, especially someone you might previously have forgotten. You must look at everyone and their opinions to see if those comments have you backed into a cage. This cage, by the way, has a name: Hidden Acting Agenda.

> **CA-7:** **What have acting teachers told me about how I come across?**
>
> **CA-7a:** **What did I change as a result?**

> **CA-8:** **What have casting people told me about how I come across?**
>
> **CA-8a:** **What did I change as a result?**

> **CA-9:** **What have directors told me about how I come across?**
>
> **CA-9a:** **What did I change as a result?**

> **CA-10:** **What has my agent told me about how I come across?**
>
> **CA-10a:** **What did I change as a result?**

> **CA-11:** **What have producers told me about how I come across?**
>
> **CA-11a:** **What did I change as a result?**

CA-12: What have audience reactions told me about how I come across?

CA-12a: What did I change as a result?

What the audience tells you might be the most important information of all. Even critics' negative reviews mean nothing if the audience likes the show and fills the theater.

CA-13: What have acting teachers told me that I needed to work on?

CA-13a: What did I change as a result?

CA-14: What have casting people told me that I needed to work on?

CA-14a: What did I change as a result?

CA-15: What have directors told me that I needed to work on?

CA-15a: What did I change as a result?

CA-16: What has my agent told me that I needed to work on?

CA-16a: What did I change as a result?

CA-17: What have producers told me that I needed to work on?

CA-17a: What did I change as a result?

CA-18: What choice have I been told didn't work, causing me to abandon that choice?

CA-19: What choice have I told myself didn't work, causing me to abandon that choice?

CA-20: What did I really have fun doing, but was told that it wasn't interesting, good, necessary or proper for good acting, so I stopped doing it?

People will change almost anything to be acceptable, except their personal habits, even though it's these life habits that may be annoying to others. That said, actors should not eliminate acting choices because it causes irritation to others in day-to-day living. That very quality might be exactly what brings a character to life. So, before you change anything, try it out in front of an audience as part of a character.

CA-21: What would I really like to work on again or for the first time?

Read over your answers from CA-7 to CA-21 and make sure you have answered the following:

CA-22: Did I change or decide anything because of feelings?

CA-23: What did I tell myself about how I come across?

CA-23a: What did I change as a result?

CA-24: What did I tell myself I needed to work on?

CA-24a: What did I change as a result?

CA-25: What opinions do I have about myself?

CA-25a: Do they help or hinder how I come across?

CA-25b: Where did they come from?

CA-25c: What did I change as a result?

CA-26: What opinions do others have about me?

CA-26a: Do they help or hinder how I come across?

CA-26b: Where did they come from?

CA-26c: What did I change as a result?

CA-27: Did I change or decide anything because of what I
told myself or convinced myself of based only on
feelings?

Now review each answer for questions CA-7 to CA-27 and
truthfully ask yourself:

CA-28: Which of the above has become part of my Hidden
Acting Agenda and may have, or has, diminished
my acting?

"I've Been Told I'm A Type"

Many actors think being a "type" is not good, but this is not
true. Being told you are a "type" can mean you affected someone
by reminding them of a more well-known actor or a familiar
character. You can come across as a "cop-type" or a "mom-
type," which isn't bad if they are looking for a "cop" or a "mom."
You may come across in a way you never realized, and perhaps
discover a "type." Therefore, don't resist being a type, especially
when you're starting out.

Casting people sometimes typecast actors as a kind of casting
shorthand. No matter how you might be typed, you can change
minds with your audition and performance.

Sometimes you come across to others as a specific category of
character.

"T" stands for Type

T-1: What type(s) have I been told I am?

T-1a: What does that mean to me?

T-1b: Do I agree with being that type(s)?

T-1c: Have I tried to prove or disprove that
type(s)?

T-1d: Is that a Hidden Acting Agenda?

Examine how any evaluations of type have affected you and what thoughts or actions you decided on as a result.

T-2: Have I been told I am better for comedy?

T-2a: What does that mean to me?

T-2b: Do I agree with that?

T-2c: Have I tried to prove or disprove that type?

T-2d: Is that a Hidden Acting Agenda?

T-3: Have I been told I am better for drama?

T-3a: What does that mean to me?

T-3b: Do I agree with that?

T-3c: Have I tried to prove or disprove that type,
and is that a Hidden Acting Agenda?

Acting Preparation

An audition or performance should be planned just as you would plan a meal. In the kitchen you refer to a cookbook or recipe to see what ingredients you'll need to concoct the meal. In your acting, you will refer to The Actor's Menu to find the ingredients you will use to create the character's story.

Aristotle believed that all human actions were either noble or base. By noble, he meant high moral qualities and by base, he meant lowly and despicable. For Aristotle, the source of any action stemmed from the moral qualities of a person.

Preparing to act means connecting with your inner characteristics or ingredients. One actor I knew would go outside, stand on the curb and bark at cars before doing his scene. I don't recommend it for everyone, but it worked for him.

We'll address actions in more detail later. I mention it now to explain that you should include all actions, whether noble or base, good or bad, as you answer the following questions. An action, whether physical, mental or behavioral, comes from character—good or bad. If you have a Hidden Acting Agenda, your preparation may be corrupted to some degree.

Whether you are a working actor wanting to improve, or an actor wanting to work, each of your acting components should be reviewed. Examine what you do in order to validate, strengthen or identify what isn't working so that you can discover what does work.

The way you approach your work is very revealing. There is no right way to prepare for an audition or performance. Let's take a close look at your preparation.

"AP" stands for Acting Preparation

AP- 1: **What truths or "rules" do I hold to concerning acting?**

AP-1a: **Is this from a feeling or from feedback?**

AP- 2: **What beliefs do I have about acting?**

AP-2a: **Is this from a feeling or from feedback?**

AP- 3: **What style of acting do I use?**

AP-3a: **Is this from a feeling or from feedback?**

AP- 4: **What do I know for a fact about acting?**

AP-4a: **Is this from a feeling or from feedback?**

AP- 5: **What am I good at as an actor?**

AP-5a: **Is this from a feeling or from feedback?**

AP- 6: What do I believe I can do as an actor?

> AP-6a: Is this from a feeling or from feedback?

AP- 7: What facts about my acting do I know?

> AP-7a: Is this from a feeling or from feedback?

AP- 8: What fact do I know about my acting, but won't tell anyone?

AP- 9: How do I prepare to perform?

AP-10: What vocal exercises do I go through?

AP-11: What physical exercises do I go through?

AP-12: Which of the above has become part of my Hidden Acting Agenda?

This is the time to be honest and examine what you really do.

Booking The Job

Booking an acting job is what you desire, but you must know what you do that makes a strong impression on the casting people, so that you can repeat it. Concentrate more on what it takes to get the job rather than with landing the job. "I booked the gig!" you declare effusively, yet you may be unaware of what you did. Knowing how you impress casting people should be your primary concern in an audition.

Auditions

A- 1: What do I do before an audition?

A- 2: What do I really think or tell myself before an audition?

A- 3: What do I expect in an audition?

A- 4: What do I believe will get me the part?

A- 5: What do I want to hear in an audition?

A- 6: What do I hear in an audition?
 A- 6a: How has that affected me?

A- 7: What do I really think as they tape me?

A- 8: Do I act insincere in an audition?
 A-8a: Why?

A- 9: What things—including attitudes—have I changed because of what I "felt" or "thought" about my work in an audition?

A-10: Did I change or decide anything because of feelings?

A-11: Which of the above has become part of my Hidden Acting Agenda?

The Work

Being a working actor means having a job in some production. Yet many actors call themselves working actors even when not cast in anything. These actors feel reluctant to admit they are someone "working to become an actor."

The real work of an actor is the constant effort to grow and develop, and should include every aspect of an actor's life. Jobs are wonderful, but without the developmental work, a job may be only a hope. That said, we'll now look at when you were actually on stage or on set, as well as offstage or off the set.

In a Scene

Before a scene or performance you may intend to do one thing but during the performance you may do another. When performing you may flinch from what you planned to do. This change is often unnatural or incomplete. Be aware of what you do when performing.

"SC" stands for Scene

SC-1: Do I become weaker or stronger when I am on stage?

SC-2: Do I pay attention to the audience?

SC-3: Do I really listen to the other actor?

Remember, listening isn't just training your eyes on another person. Listening isn't just hearing the words. Even though the definition of listening is to make an effort to hear or to pay attention, that isn't really listening. Listening is connecting what the other person is saying to your experience, your beliefs, your truths. Listening in a scene means being affected and, if you are not, you must create the connection from the other actor's words to your personal knowledge.

SC-4: **Do I block out what I don't like or disagree with?**

SC-5: **Do I prevent others' ideas from affecting me?**

SC-6: **Do I "feel" like I'm someone else?**
> SC-6a: **Is this caused by a Hidden Acting Agenda?**

When in a scene and faced with some part of your Hidden Acting Agenda, you may unknowingly revert to your Hidden Acting Agenda. Identifying your Hidden Acting Agenda helps you gain control over it. Acting, bringing a character to life, may require that you discomfort yourself in order to be true to the character.

SC-7: **Do I try to be comfortable and avoid being uncomfortable when I am in a scene?**
> SC-7a: **Is this caused by a Hidden Acting Agenda?**

SC-8: **Do I experience pleasant or unpleasant physical or mental reactions to performing?**
> SC-8a: **Is this caused by a Hidden Acting Agenda?**

SC-9: **Am I only thinking about my next line?**

SC-10: **Do I feel alive, strong and free when I'm in a scene?**

Being uncomfortable, hearing every noise the audience makes, focusing on the audience and not being yourself are not good. These distractions come from Hidden Acting Agendas, and you need to verify whether the source is opinion or experience.

Plays•Movies•Industrials•Commercials

With each of the following sets of questions, consider carefully every possible area for your acting successes and your acting problems. These questions should bring to mind the times you were validated or invalidated for your performances.

"**P**" stands for Plays, "**M**" stands for Movies, "**I**" for Industrials and "**C**" for Commercials.

Plays

List each play by name and each character by type.

Example: I appeared in (name of the play). My role was that of (describe the character). Or, I was a soldier in two scenes with no dialogue.

P-1: **What plays have I been in?**

P-2: **What characters have I portrayed?**

P-3: **What was I told about my performances?**

   P-3a: **By whom?**

   P-3b: **Did that critique become part of my Hidden Acting Agenda?**

P-4: **What feedback did I get from this performance?**

P-5: **What reviews did I get?**

   P-5a: **Have those reviews become a part of my Hidden Acting Agenda?**

P-6: **What did I learn from this experience?**

P-7: **What did you change as a result of this feedback?**

P-8: Did I change or decide anything because of my own perception of my performance without regard of outside evidence?

The above questions include feedback from directors. It is perfectly all right for you to evaluate a director's critique. Some direction can contain hidden evaluations that can affect you negatively. If that was the case, you may have experienced thoughts like these after the play: "I don't know why, but I feel like giving up acting." There are times when a negative comment can motivate you into trying harder.

Consider a director's comments beneficial if your performance improves. But if the comment makes you lose faith in yourself or feel like abandoning your dreams, it is not constructive. Dismiss it. It won't help you.

Movies

M- 1: What feature movies have I appeared in?

M- 2: What characters did I portray?

M- 3: What did I learn from each experience?

M- 4: What feedback did I get?

M-4a: From whom?

M-4b: Did that feedback become part of my Hidden Acting Agenda?

M- 5: What reviews did I receive?

M- 5a: From whom?

M- 6: What did I change as a result?

M- 7: What student movies have I appeared in?

M- 8: What characters did I portray?

M- 9: What did I learn from these experiences?

M-10: What feedback did I get?
>   M-10a: From whom?
>
>   M-10b: Did that experience become part of my
>   Hidden Acting Agenda?

M-11: What reviews did I receive?
>   M-11a: From whom?

M-12: What did I change as a result of the review?

M-13: What shorts have I appeared in?

M-14: What characters did I portray?

M-15: What did I learn from appearing in the movie
or short?
>   M-15a: Has that become part of my Hidden
>   Acting Agenda?

M-16: What feedback did I get?
>   M-16a: From whom?

M-17: What reviews did I receive?
>   M-17a: From whom?

M-18: What have I changed as a result?

M-19: Did I change or decide anything because of
my feelings?

Industrials

I-1: What industrial films or videos have I appeared in?

I-2: What characters did I portray?

I-3: What did I learn from these experiences?

    I-3a: Did that become part of my Hidden Acting Agenda?

I-4: What feedback did I get?

I-5: What reviews did I receive?

I- 6: What have I changed as a result?

I- 7: Did I change or decide anything because of feelings?

Commercials

C- 1: What commercials have I appeared in?

C- 2: What characters did I portray?

C- 3: What did I learn from these experiences?

C- 4: What feedback did I get?

C- 5: What reviews did I receive?

    C- 5a: Did they become part of my Hidden Acting Agenda?

C- 6: What did I change as a result?

C- 7: Did I change or decide anything because of my feelings?

On The Job

"J" stands for Job.

J- 1: What are my routine actions when I arrive on the set?

J- 2: When rehearsals start, do I show what I think or wait to be told?

J- 2a: Why?

J- 3: Am I intimidated by the crew?

J- 4: Am I intimidated by the director?

J- 5: Am I intimidated by the cast?

J- 6: Am I intimidated by the stage or set?

J- 7: If I have been intimidated, how did that affect my work?

J- 8: Do I think that if I uncover my feelings, they will be negated?

J- 9: When I get to the stage or the set, do I feel excited and ready to go?

J-10: Do I feel confident enough to give my thoughts honestly to the director?

J-11: Do I work my choices in the rehearsal?

J-12: Do I back off in any way for any reason?

J-13: Did I decide on actions or attitudes because of my own feelings?

J-14: Have I created an item for my Hidden Acting Agenda from these experiences?

Training

For the answers in the following sections, do not make the kind of list that you would include on your résumé. Make this a list of what you actually learned and were told. For example, students who take acting courses in college often learn more outside the class, while appearing in or working on productions. Experience teaches. Learn from the audience's response when you apply the information learned in a class.

Training as an actor must include working with emotions, feelings and attitudes.

Let's look at your structured experience in acting classes or workshops.

Acting Class

Acting classes are where you discover your acting. You must attend several sessions of any class before deciding if that class is for you, and, you must not make decisions based on other people's opinions about that class.

Galileo summed up what I believe to be the true purpose of an acting class when he said: "You cannot teach a man anything; you can only help him find it within himself."

The best lessons are obtained through the audience, revealing how you came across, and then through what adjustments you make based on that feedback.

In Greek and Roman drama, a *deus ex machina* was a god introduced to resolve the plot entanglements. An acting class is not a place where a magical deus ex machina will arrive, to solve your acting problems. An acting class is a place for you to present your work and develop, not a place to find an answer that resolves your acting confusions.

"AC" stands for Acting Class.

AC- 1: **What do I want from an acting class?**
AC-1a: **Why?**

AC- 2: **I have joined or would join an acting class:**
- **because of the teacher's or the class's reputation**
- **after auditing the class**
- **because of the attractive people in the class**
- **because a friend told me to join**
- **some other reason (and if so, what?)**

AC- 3: **Was my decision not to join a class made because of any Hidden Acting Agendas?**

AC- 4: **What reasons do I have for not joining a class?**
Consider these answers:
- **I heard it was too tough**
- **I heard it was too easy**
- **I heard bad things**
- **I didn't like the ad**

- I didn't like the look of the building
- I didn't like the look of the teacher
- I didn't like what they did when I attended some classes
- I audited the class and I just had a "feeling."

Some of these choices may have been made because of Hidden Acting Agendas.

Class Time

If you have been in an acting class, review your experience.

AC- 5: Do I take notes?

AC- 6: Do I work in class?

AC- 7: Do I agree with what I am told about my acting?

AC- 8: How do I react to feedback if it's positive?

AC- 9: How do I react to feedback if it's negative?

AC-10: How much time do I spend working on my assignments?

AC-11: Do I wait until the last moment to prepare?

AC-12: Do I see people change?

AC-13: Do I understand what is going on?

AC-14: Do I often change classes?

　　　　AC-14a: Why?

AC-15: What am I really looking for in a class?

AC-16: Does what I am told to do agree with what I think?

AC-16a: If not, specifically why not?

AC-16b: If not, why am I still in this class?

AC-16c: If so, is it because I don't have a clear point of view?

AC-17: Has the class changed my mind about what I think?

AC-18: Have I been able to see or understand the result of my beliefs?

AC-19: Have I changed something about my acting without seeing if it worked in class?

AC-20: Have I decided not to change something because it was suggested that it was a good idea to change?

Sometimes you may be advised to change some attitude or behavior not because it's wrong but because the advisor wants to steal that attitude or behavior, or because it offends his or her own Hidden Acting Agenda.

AC-21: Why am I in a class?

AC-22: Have I changed or decided anything regarding acting classes because of feelings and not experience?

AC-23: Has a Hidden Acting Agenda been formed from these classes?

AC-23a: If so, detail what and how that is helping or hindering my acting.

AC-24: Did I choose a class because of a Hidden Acting Agenda?

AC-25: Does the feedback I receive tell me how I came
across or what I should do?

AC-25a: How do I feel about that feedback?

If being told how to act makes you feel good, you should ask
yourself if this is a Hidden Acting Agenda. That Hidden Acting
Agenda can prevent you from having your own opinions when
they differ and upset others.

Reading

Reading screenplays and plays develops your ability to
experience images, thoughts and imagination. Also, scripts,
plays or screenplays require a different reading skill, as they are
not written in prose and give a different impression than one
might get from a book.

"R" stands for Reading

R-1: How many plays have I read?

R-2: How many screenplays have I read?

If your answer is "not many," start reading scripts—any scripts,
all scripts. Free up your imagination and your ideas.

R-3: How many novels have I read?

R-4: What do I like to read?

R-4a: Does my reading feed my acting?

Be sure to read what fuels your acting. A script can do that, as
can a novel or a biography.

R-5: What writers move me?

R-5a: Why?

R-6: What writers bother me?

R-6a: Why?

Exclude as little as possible from your study. The book, play or script you don't read may contain the impression that will enhance your acting menu.

Writing

One way to better understand characters is to write them. Whether or not you have written a script, you should write characters to understand characters, if not to actually write a script or book. First, write a one page scene, then two. Then, get someone to act out your scene and see how it communicates.

"W" stands for Writing

W-1: What plays, movies or scenes have I written?

W-1a: Were they performed?

W-1b: What was the feedback?

W-1c: What did I learn?

W-1d: What did I change in my acting as a result?

W-1e: Is that change part of my Hidden Acting Agenda?

W-2: What characters have I written?

W-2a: What was the feedback?

W-2b: What did I learn?

W-2c: What did I change in my acting as a result?

W-2d: **Is that change part of my Hidden Acting Agenda?**

Feedback such as "You're not a funny person" doesn't mean you can't write comedy. It means you keep working at it, if you want to make people laugh. You not only find your *writing voice* by writing, you can also find your *actor's voice*.

W-3: **Did I change or decide anything because of feelings or feedback?**

Keep an ongoing acting journal. It's interesting to look back from time-to-time and see if you changed something because of a comment that wasn't in your best interest after all. Write down what you have learned or discovered after every class and performance–especially what you have changed as a result of the feedback and the experience.

Real development emerges from what you discover about yourself. Your journal will help you keep track of how you come across and how and where you received the information.

Dance/Movement

Movement is important and should be understood. Why? For one reason, young people don't move the same as older people. A lame person moves differently than someone with full mobility. You need to know how to move convincingly for each role.

"D" stands for Dance/Movement

D-1: **What dance training have I had?**

D-2: **What movement training have I had?**

D-3: **How do I move?**

D-4: How is my posture?

D-5: What have I been told about my dancing ability?

D-6: What did I change as a result of this feedback?

D-7: Did I change or decide anything because of my feelings?

Voice

Vocal technique is too often omitted from an actor's training. Singers aren't the only talent who need to understand voice production. To endure nights of rehearsals and performances, you need to study breathing and voice. Warming up your voice in the shower is a great place because there is much less stress on the vocal instrument. And since you have to shower anyway, there is no excuse for not having the time to warm up.

"V" stands for Voice

V-1: What voice training have I had?

V-2: What evaluation did I get about my voice?

V-3: What vocal exercises do I do?

V-4: What have I been told about my voice?

V-5: What did I change as a result of this information?

V-6: Did I change or decide anything concerning my voice because of "feelings" I had while performing?

Scripts

Actors often have attitudes about scripts. Whether you like or dislike a script you've been given, the script is the structure for your performance. A good actor can usually improve an inferior script. When you get a script, don't let negative opinions about the script alter your performance, especially while you are a beginning actor. If you get what you consider to be a "bad" script, you can still learn something from it as you work to tell the story. A script is a script, but what you do with it can make all the difference.

"S" stands for Scripts

S-1: What do I do when I get a script, sides or a scene?

S-2: How do I read it?

    S-2a: In one sitting?

    S-2b: In between other things?

S-3: Do I think positive or negative thoughts as I'm reading?

S-4: When do I decide whether I like or don't like what I'm reading?

S-5: How many scripts of plays and movies have I read?

S-6: What scripts do I like?

    S-6a: Why?

S-7: Do I like scripts because of the story or because of a character I could play?

S-8: What do I think I have to do if I don't like the script?

S-9: What do I think the elements of a good script are?

S-10: Do I decide anything about the script because of my feelings?

S-11: Were any of the above decisions the result of a Hidden Acting Agenda?

If you hate a script you will be performing, don't hide these feelings. Make four copies. Tramp on and kick the first copy, while screaming how bad it is. Line the bottom of a trash can with the second one. Tear the third copy to shreds with your hands, venting contempt and hatred for the script. This should exorcise most of the negativity. Now, free of the negative feelings, get to work creating the story.

Your Process

You likely have an external process, such as reading the script to find the objective—who is talking, what are they talking about and what is really going on. Well and good, but what is your internal process?

Possibly you aren't aware of your internal steps. It's good to discover what internal steps you actually take. Your Hidden Acting Agenda is part of your process and acts like a filter or a converter that alters anything that is related to that item. If your process is set up to "protect" you from any and all perceived flaws or weirdness, it's totally in opposition to becoming an affecting actor.

"P" stands for Process

For questions P-1 through P-4, look for internal actions or inactions, such as doubting you can do it, criticizing the script, not experiencing the script and not noting any impulses or ideas. It's important for you to know what your process is, whether conscious or not.

P-1: **What internal steps do I go through when I get a script, scene or side, from the first read until I start to memorize?**

P-2: **What do I think about as I go through a script or scene I will be performing?**

P-3: **What steps and thoughts do I go through when I read a script or scene I will be performing?**

P-4: **What do I do with feelings that come up while I'm reading a script or scene I will be performing?**

P-5: **What do I do with ideas or impulses I get while I am reading a script or scene I will be performing?**

P-6: **What do I experience when reading a script or scene I will be performing?**

P-7: **How many times do I read a script or scene I will be performing?**

P-8: **What do I actually do when I work on a script or scene I will be performing?**

P-9: **What are the sources of my current process?**

Take some time with this section. Examine your thoughts as you read, memorize and prepare to perform. Until you break up the syntax of your process, you won't effectively change what you are doing. In the kitchen, you would clean out the bowl before mixing new and different ingredients. In your acting, be aware of the ingredients you are including when creating your character.

An Exercise:

Select a short monologue you have not read before. Have paper and pen ready.

Sit down and start to read it. Every time you have a thought, any thought, write it down. This includes negative thoughts, thoughts about balancing the checkbook, any and all thoughts. Stop reading and write them down when they occur. Then, when you have finished reading the monologue, read the thoughts you had. Circle the thoughts that had to do with performing the monologue.

You might find you had many thoughts or ideas that wouldn't help create the monologue. These distracting thoughts are road-bumps on your process and make creating a character presentation more problematic. Being unaware of them could mean that they will affect your impression of the script. For instance, reading a love story could be tainted by thoughts of your last painful breakup.

Clearing The Table

Clearing the table is about starting fresh. It can be done after the main course before the dessert, or anytime before a new course. These next questions will help you clean up any overlooked ideas and thoughts you may have about your acting.

"**CT**" stands for Clearing the Table

CT- 1: **What do I hate doing as an actor?**

CT- 1a: **Did my Hidden Acting Agenda cause this?**

CT- 2: What am I most afraid of as an actor?

> CT- 2a: Did my Hidden Acting Agenda cause this?

CT- 3: What am I most afraid of while acting?

> CT- 3a: Did my Hidden Acting Agenda cause this?

CT- 4: What negative thoughts or actions do I have before, during or after performing?

> CT- 4a: Has this affected my work?

> CT- 4b: Did my Hidden Acting Agenda cause this?

CT- 5: What do I really like to do as an actor?

> CT- 5a: Do I do it?

> CT- 5b: Why or why not?

CT- 6: What is the most pleasurable part of acting or being an actor?

CT- 7: When I'm acting, what do I do that gets the best response?

CT- 8: Have I ever changed or decided anything solely based on "feelings?"

A Flinch Test

A few more questions, just to be sure you didn't miss or flinch
from anything. Flinching, backing away, is the first part of
a sequence that goes: flinch, default. The default, just after
an actor flinches, is a predetermined action that is employed
automatically to activate a Hidden Acting Agenda. The default
after a flinch is also done to protect an actor from having to face
something challenging or threatening.

"FT" stands for Flinch Test

FT- 1: **What thoughts do I have when challenged?**

FT- 1a: **Who or what was the source of those
thoughts?**

FT- 1b: **Do I want these thoughts to be part of
my process?**

FT- 2: **What actions do I think, believe or feel I must do
when performing?**

FT- 2a: **Do I want these to be a part of my
process?**

FT- 3: **What behaviors do I think, believe or feel I must do
when performing?**

FT- 3a: **Do I want these to be a part of my
process?**

FT- 4: **What emotions do I think, believe or feel I must do
when performing?**

FT- 4a: **Do I want these to be a part of my
process?**

FT- 5: **What actions do I think, believe or feel I must not
do when performing?**

FT- 5a: **How did I determine each of these?**

FT- 5b: What was its original source?

FT- 5c: Do I want these to be a part of my
process?

FT- 6: What behaviors do I think, believe or feel I must
not do when performing?

FT- 6a: How did I determine each of these?

FT- 6b: What was its original source?

FT- 6c: Do I want these to be a part of my
process?

FT- 7: What emotions do I think, believe or feel I must not
show when performing?

FT- 7a: How did I determine each of these?

FT- 7b: What was its original source?

FT- 7c: Do I want these to be a part of my
process?

FT- 8: What do I do in auditions or any acting work in
spite of what I have been told is best for me?

FT- 8a: Do I want these to be a part of my
process?

This is the end of the Appetizer section of this handbook. If you
think of anything not listed, add the question and answer it.

Since this section, like a good appetizer, should stimulate the
desire for more, your answers, at the very least, should tweak
your interest in what you can do to create the very best Actor's
Menu, free from Hidden Acting Agendas or any other agendas.

Now, on to the Entrée!

Entrée

The word *entrée* has different meanings. It's the main course of a meal, but it also means the opening of new opportunities. We'll use both senses of the word in this handbook. This entrée, this main course, will open up your potential, resulting in a list of ingredients or choices from which you will form your Actor's Menu.

Chefs strive for individuality in their approach and presentation. For actors, menus should be a limitless, detailed listing of individual personal choices that have been tested in front of an audience.

This main course is the heart of The Actor's Menu. The Actor's Menu is the series of actions that result in your Acting Menu. This final menu is the list of choices you offer, but only after those choices have proven to be effective.

The time it takes to prepare a dinner far exceeds the time it takes to appreciate the presentation or consume the meal. The preparation is the work. You rehearse a play for weeks or months and one presentation lasts a couple of hours, with intermission. You learn your part in a film and it lasts for 20 seconds of screen time. Regardless of the time spent, having others participate in a meal or a performance and having their palates excited and their senses satisfied is the reward.

Preparing an exciting meal requires a good knowledge of the ingredients. The entrée section in this handbook covers the major ingredients of an actor's creation. You will find that you may not have fully understood some of these ingredients. It's time to clear that up.

In acting, the work of preparing and presenting a character that entices, stimulates and satisfies an audience's emotions and intellec, is an actor's true joy. A performance, like a meal, is nothing without an audience. Finally, it is the response from these involved participants that determines the success of the presentation and thus the wisdom of the choices.

Primary Ingredients

Characters are made up of many individual ingredients, just like you.

No chef limits a dish to just one ingredient—a plate of cabbage would satisfy only a rabbit. The same is true with your work as an actor. You won't rely on one ingredient but will develop and include different ingredients, different elements.

Your ingredients are the character's ingredients. That means that you will be discovering and developing your own ingredients, including them in your work as you complete your actor's menu.

Be very curious as you go through the following ingredients. Don't accept or reject what you read without confirmation that it does or doesn't work for you. To that end, there is an old saying: Trust, but verify. This is the core of The Actor's Menu concept. When you choose an element, trust that if you fully perform that choice, it will work. Then, confirm it by the audience's feedback.

The ingredients listed in this section are vital. Without them no character recipe could exist. Don't shut your mind and assume you know them because they are so "obvious." Trust you know them, but verify that you do know them.

You'll need the following ingredients to create a rich, vibrant character. There are elements that you possess and if you want to add them, do so. After all, The Actor's Menu will result in your personal, potent acting menu.

You

"To be nobody-but-yourself—in a world which is doing its best, night and day, to make you everybody else— means to fight the hardest battle which any human being can fight; and never stop fighting."

                                               –e.e. cummings

You will discover more and more about the battle it takes to be yourself throughout this handbook, your acting career and your life. Making these discoveries requires a willingness to be open to all of your impulses, thoughts and quirks.

"Do I Have Talent?"

That is the one question all actors rethink at various times, usually after a bad audition or performance. To many actors, a negative answer to this question means they should give up acting. (Why proceed with a dream to act if the answer is no?) A positive reply means to go ahead with the dream.

Talent is generally thought of as natural ability. However, another meaning for talent is desire. So, when you ask, "Do I have talent?" are you trying to determine if you have a natural ability or the hunger to succeed?

Concerning acting, I think of natural ability as a "gift." Such gifts could be the ability to hear and repeat sounds on an instrument, be it a violin or their own vocal cords or the ability to present a moving and affecting character without training or coaching.

To me, the real question you should ask yourself is: "Do I have the desire to become an actor?" If you are willing to use everything that you are, all your ingredients, to become an actor, you have all the talent you need.

This now gives you two questions. "Do I have a gift?" or "Do I have the desire?" Each can be answered but the most important question concerns desire. Desire and persistence often give rise to what many see as natural ability. Persistence is essential in any career.

In this handbook, when I say "talent" I am referring to your desire. The desire to succeed is no more important than the desire to discover your ingredients.

The intensity of the need and the desire to tell a story can be the deciding factor in whether you "make it" or not. And to that person who warned you, "You'll never make it as an actor," talent can even be that hunger to prove them wrong. (See, Payback page 28.)

You are setting out on a venture laden with risk. Whether you intend to discover more about yourself, develop better acting skills or are just beginning the adventure of acting you are taking the risk of revealing yourself. For many actors putting yourself "out there" as you must do in an audition or in a performance is considered the biggest risk.

This risk means revealing personal thoughts about yourself, such as ideas that you feel are different and offbeat. This risk of putting yourself "out there" can also expose that one scary thought which is the worst of all—the thought that you don't have any talent. The truth is, personal idiosyncrasies and fears, when presented in the context of a character, are seen by an audience as indication of the actor's talent. You must risk bringing every part of who you are to your acting.

Sooner or later you will leave the comfort of home and venture out into the big world. In doing so you risk failure, among other things. Acting is never a safe, comfortable activity. Auditioning is never without risk and stress. Opening nights are never approached without trepidation. Making any acting choice is chancy, unless you believe in yourself.

View your acting as a challenge to reveal your deeply held traits and behaviors. Include theses traits and behaviors in your performance, in order to affect the character and the audience. Everyone feels apprehensive as they undertake an acting career, especially when they have to "reveal themselves." Yet that is the challenge for an actor—telling the complete story of the character. It's a challenge that you can meet if you are well prepared.

Every time I'm asked, "Do you think I have the talent to be an actor?" My answer is always, "If you have the desire!"

I have selected some quotes to reinforce this point about talent. Consider them before you move on.

"It took me fifteen years to discover I had no talent for writing, but I couldn't give it up because by then I was too famous."

–Robert Benchley

"Use what talents you possess: the woods would be very silent if no birds sang there except those that sang best."

–Henry Van Dyke

"Patience and perseverance have a magical effect before which difficulties disappear and obstacles vanish."

–John Quincy Adams

"Beyond talent lie all the usual words: discipline, love, luck —but, most of all, endurance."

–James Baldwin

"Everyone has talent. What is rare is the courage to follow the talent to the dark place where it leads."

–Erica Jong

View your talent as your passion to affect others, to reveal a character, to tell a story, and, thereby, to further discover your abilities. Persist. And use rejection as the motivation to prove wrong those who denied you.

Imagination

"Imagination is the beginning of creation. You imagine what you desire, you will what you imagine and at last you create what you will."

–George Bernard Shaw

Imagination is inherent within you. However, this ingredient needs to be clearly defined before assuming its place in the mix.

Imagination is a combination of what has been observed and also what has never been seen, which is blended with present events and things. Imagination consists in taking parts of existing images and combining them into new mixes more striking, more delightful and more terrible than those of everyday experience.

Imagination is the creative part of the mind where new ideas, thoughts and images are formed. It's the ability to create new ways of dealing with situations, difficulties or problems. Imagination is found in dreams, resourcefulness, ingenuity, creativity, powers of invention, and inspiration.

To dream is to imagine. The diarist, Anais Nin, wrote, "Dreams pass into the reality of action. From the action stems the dream again; and this interdependence produces the highest form of living."

Your imagination is the ingredient that connects dreams to action. Your dream of creating a great character will come to life as it passes through your imagination.

One way to get started creating a character is to take an event from a script and ask, "How could I do that?" Then, let your imagination go to work. The result may startle, please or scare you, but usually it is good for a character.

If you become tense or nervous about creating new and fresh characters, you have discovered another acting problem. If, however, you are excited to risk creating new realities, you will alleviate many acting problems.

You might fear that doing this will offend the writer or director. In fact, the life you bring to your performance may enhance the character beyond what the writer had imagined.

Your imagination is your unique point of view that distinguishes you from all others. Use it to combine ingredients never before combined in that way. Imagination is power.

Example:

```
EXT. Street Night
A woman walks into a parking lot and suddenly
stops.

                    WOMAN
            Who's there?
```

The above excerpt tells you little. You add what's important. You could let the character realize something is wrong, increase the fear, and add a laugh to cover. Or allow the character to realize that it was just her imagination. Now you try to add in your own ideas using the same example, but don't omit any wild, strange images you get.

The character stops, turns and says, "Who's there?" The next step requires imagination.

The character could_____(you fill in the blank)

or the character could_____(you fill in the blank)

It's that easy. Characters who come alive have always traveled through the actor's imagination. Act from the depth of your imagination. Act to celebrate, to discover, to mourn. Act from your pains, and your flaws, not your Hidden Acting Agendas. Do that and it will be art. Try to present art, without a deep connection, and it will fall short. Be willing to discover what is deep within you.

In a world where you are goaded to resemble others, your imagination is your guiding star. As was once said, the theater is a safe place to do (imagine) unsafe things. If liberating your imagination is perilous to you, find a way to explore that wonderful world gradually.

George Bernard Shaw's famous quote applies well to actors working to discover a character: "You see things and you say, 'Why?' But I dream things that never were and say, 'Why not?'"

Some Words About Words

Before the story was the word. And words that are not fully understood or effectively used often defeat a story. Actors, like most people, make assumptions about the meanings and definitions of words, often to avoid a hidden agenda. Not fully understanding the meaning of words can derail your progress or numb an affecting performance. Make a dictionary a vital part of your acting career; look up every word you don't know.

Words can excite, motivate, offend, hurt or gladden. If the words don't have an effect on your ideas, thoughts or feelings, or you don't understand what they mean, how will you affect an audience?

Words can provide references to an image, a thought. They are mental entities that trigger the contents of the image. Words have power because of what they mean to the person who hears or reads them.

Each word has two senses, the denotative and the connotative. The denotative meaning is basically the explicit definition you find in a dictionary. For example, *birthday* is defined as *the anniversary of one's birth*. Then there is the connotative meaning. This is the flavor of the word. It is the image or feeling in the mind that occurs in response to hearing or reading the word. You could say that this is the subtext of the denotative meaning. With the word *birthday* the connotative meaning could be "I'm getting older!" The word *audition* is defined *as a test or trial of the performer* but the connotative meaning too often is: "Fear."

This difference is important because connotative meanings of words are what affect the audience. You can vary the connotative meaning of a word that describes a character and, in doing so, change a character.

It's only the connotative meaning of a word that has strong emotional content. It's the connotative meaning that makes people listen. People think in emotion, symbols and images, not definitions.

When you are inventing a character you must use words that have a strong meaning for you, even if the word makes no sense to anyone else. It is your response to the words that will affect the audience.

Fuzzy Words

Another important classification to note is the distinction between fuzzy and concrete words. A fuzzy word is a word or phrase that is deliberately confusing or euphemistic. Fuzzy words are those words that do not indicate anything specific. "Success" is a fuzzy word. Success means different things to different people. Another fuzzy word, "justice," can mean anything from a jury's decision to a vendetta. Fuzzy words are ineffective because they lead to fuzzy acting choices.

Concrete words refer to definite items. That is, you can point at an example of what you mean by that word, as in: scream, laugh, sit, stand, push, throw. Actors want words that conjure up strong meanings, ideas and specific connotations. It isn't the word, but the meaning that affects the audience.

Often scripts use words that are fuzzy and not specific as to the character's intention or feeling. Saying a character is "upset" can be fuzzy if there are no other words to clarify the emotion that is wanted. *Upset* can mean *perturbed* or *completely deranged*. A concrete way of describing exactly what kind of "upset" is wanted is: "She's sad, quiet, slow moving" or "She's full of rage, throwing items, screaming in a fit."

Notes given by directors can be fuzzy. For example, "He's vulgar, I want vulgarity," "She's unrefined, unpolished." Or the most famous of directions, "Give me more energy." These kinds of fuzzy notes can leave an actor confused and wondering exactly what to do.

If you are confused by a word or description, determine if it **is** fuzzy and if so, make it specific, even if you have to ask the director for clarification. For example, when you are told, "more energy is needed," look for the emotion involved and heighten it. The same goes with "more upset." The word *more* indicates a higher level and, so increase the level of the turmoil.

Words can make people react, behave and think in certain ways. Obviously, some words create predictable reactions such as: *mother, son, failure, audition,* or *dentist.* By choosing words according to their denotative and connotative meanings, you can increase or decrease their impact.

Story

Telling stories comes naturally to human beings. We can't stop telling stories. We tell stories because we want to affect people with a part of our life that has affected us. We even ask for stories: "How was your day?" "What did your folks say?" "Why don't you send me out on that audition?" The response to each of these questions is a story.

Actors in their rush to "be good" often overlook the story of a script. But the story is important.

In the history of drama, stories have been viewed from two perspectives. Plays were either plot-driven or character-driven. The Greek philosopher, Aristotle (384–322 BC) taught that plot was the first principal of drama. In his six elements of a tragic drama—plot, character, diction, thought, spectacle and melody—he list plot before character. He used this sequence because to him, drama was a portrayal of action, not character. He said character is revealed by action and reaction: good people carry out good actions; bad people carry out bad actions.

Aristotle divided actions into either voluntary or involuntary action. The cause of voluntary actions is internal and mental: deciding to travel to Europe, or to add a room to the house. The cause of involuntary actions is external: anger when you're cut off in traffic or sadness after the other actor got the part in the project.

Aristotle also stated that the fundamental demand of a story is having audiences care for the characters. The audience must identify and have pity and sympathy for the characters.

Much of Aristotle's writings are still true today, except that in modern drama character is the first principal. We remember characters more than plots.

In dictionaries the words *story* and *plot* are mentioned in each other's definitions. For some understanding, let's separate them, giving each a function from which an actor will create the character.

A story produces the chain of events and situations. Plot creates the order and connection between the events of the story. The plot line is the connection to the rising and falling of action in a story.

Here is the classic difference between story and plot, as illustrated by the British novelist E. M. Forster in *Aspects of the Novel*:

> Story: "The king died. The queen died."
> Plot: "The king died. The queen died of grief."

This popular comparison of story and plot, given in one sentence, is enough to bring forth images of the characters, especially of the queen who "died of grief."

A story gives the sequence of events, but without a plot, the audience does not know *why*. The story takes an audience on a journey of human need. The plot is the method used to advance the story toward its dramatic, potent resolution by defining the whys. The plot is used to connect the series of events. How each character acts and reacts is part of the plot, which arose from the story.

You can't affect the story but you can affect the plot, with how you create your character.

The script's story and plot takes audiences to many places and allows them to feel and think of things that are normally out of their grasp or secretly tucked away.

Your fires of creativity in acting should be ignited by story and plot. Not all scripts create fires. Some don't even make smoke. The script's power is unimportant because it's the actor's job to bring heat to the story—whether the story handed to the actor it is a blazing hot script or a script whose flame has never been ignited.

A story describes a time of life, a linear journey through adversity, conflict, challenge and other obstacles that culminates in a dramatically potent and gratifying conclusion. The audience must experience this journey.

Every story has a theme. The theme is the central idea, the unifying idea, around which the story and characters are formed. It carries the message to be conveyed. Characters have themes as well. Little Red Riding Hood's theme was: Don't talk to strangers. Macbeth's theme was: Unscrupulous ambition leads to ruin.

The Character's Story

Your job is to tell the story of a character. It's the character's story that moves and affects. Your character story must be appropriate to the script's story. Your interpretation of that story is up to you. Before you begin to work on the character, spend some time understanding the story.

Character

Some actors know what a character is, others talk as if they do. Too often a character lacks depth because the actor hasn't tapped the feast of personal ingredients that exist within the actor.

A role that an actor takes on lives within that actor. The character on the page awakens similar characteristics within that actor. Characters do not somehow transfer from page to actor, they are brought to life by the actor from within.

Actors interchange "my character" with "me" or "I." However you refer to the character, you won't be able to create a character with any ingredients other than those you possess. You can't be anyone else. You can only tell the story with what you have to offer: your voice, attitudes, mannerisms and actions. Each of your personal characteristics are what distinguish you from other actors and give your characters a unique quality.

Specific qualities and distinctive features are what make your characters. Your emotions are a distinctive feature of you, and your emotion is the character's emotion, your intention is the character's intention.

Working with actors, I have often witnessed the lack of strong character elements in their scenes and in front of a camera. This comes from not allowing the potent images they find in the story to stimulate the character ingredients they possess. If you fail to look for or realize the story's impact, you omit the first step to developing a strong character.

For an actor, the evolution of the character begins with the first reading of a script or scene. This first read-through, if you are open to it, creates an impression, which lays the groundwork for the final presentation of the character.

All characters arrive with a past (just like you), a history that has helped form who they are. This background is often seen as unnecessary baggage that encumbers a role, but it is the characters' qualities that make them human.

A character is never just a mom, a dad, a sister, a brother, a doctor or a lawyer. Those are labels and you can't act labels; you can't act a "mom," "doctor" or "soldier" because they aren't specific. Is the mom gentle or tough? Is the doctor caring or cold? Is the soldier brave or cowardly? Likely, the mom, brother or doctor you act will have the qualities of someone who affected you in the past—a real person, with all of the complexities that we, as human beings, have.

A character's point of view is revealed by their attitude and their position toward or about some subject. "She has an attitude" means she has an unexpressed or partially expressed emotion or feeling toward a person, thing or event. Attitudes are formed from experiences in the past, usually emotional events.

Characters can be round or flat, full or skimpy, one-dimensional or multi-dimensional, single-voiced or many-voiced. Flat, skimpy, one-dimensional, single-voiced characters are simply stereotypes formed without any depth. Stereotype indicates that nothing more than what we see is contained in that character.

A definition of stereotype is: one considered typical of a group, without individuality. After a superficial representation, there's nothing more to come, for example: "He's a great 'bad guy'," "She's a 'suburban housewife.'" In these stereotypes, that is all that is needed, any other character elements are not revealed.

To affect an audience, your characters should be full, rounded, multi-dimensional and many-voiced, not stereotypes but individuals, different from other individuals. They are "your mom," "the doctor who saved your life" or "your cousin, the soldier." They are specific and personal.

When you create a poignant, multi-faceted character, showing much more depth, that character ceases to be a "type."

If you have been "typed" as a character actor, you can specifically show what kind of character actor you are: deep and sensitive, loud and bullish, weak and frail. Therefore, an actor can control stereotyping. Being told "You are a comedy type" is better than being told you're not anything, but if you hate comedy, it may be the end of the road. Instead of giving up acting, maybe you should give comedy a try.

Multi-dimensional characters are full of many ingredients, physical and mental. Multi-dimensional characters are strong characters, and the only characters audiences want to see.

A word to describe this full, rich, round character is *polyphonic*, many voices speaking out. This character is like a stew, with many individual ingredients, each adding its specific quality to enhance the overall dish.

Just as a fantastic main course should excite the diner's palate, a character should excite the audience's emotional palate. Strong characters drive the action and the story.

Activities in a story are primarily carried out by characters. These actions are either internal, such as emotion, or external, such as physical behaviors.

Discovering and concocting a character requires both outward and inward observation. Sharp observation of other people and their reactions to events, large and small, creates impressions that bring out specific reactions in you.

Detailed observation also results in imaginative identification. This is where you observe a specific reaction and then enhance it with your imagination. You can glean and awaken many traits and character attitudes from watching others as they move through their lives. An actor must learn through reading people. Much of life is dependent upon perceiving others needs, strengths and weaknesses.

When I began acting, a few other actors and I had a way of testing our observation skills. We would get on a bus and study a passenger without him knowing it. We would try to determine if the person was married, single or divorced; what kind of job they did; whether they had children; and what hobbies they had.

To verify our findings, we would approach the person and tell him or her we were conducting an exercise for our acting class and would be grateful for a "yes" or "no" answer to our observations. Over time, through trial and error, we were rewarded with more and more "yes" answers.

Introspection

When I use the word "introspection," I mean internal observation. For some, introspection might seem unpleasant. Goethe said: "If you start to think about your physical or moral condition, you usually find out you are sick." And you might well find your dark as well as your light side during your self-examination.

An actor who is unwilling to discover that he is "cursed" with a personality weakness may deny a character a vital ingredient that makes that character personal and individual. Introspection doesn't mean chastising yourself for sins. It means to openly, honestly and bravely perceive yourself. Inward observation must be truthful and courageous.

Some of the attributes you find in yourself may be quirky or odd. Actors often avoid their quirks out of embarrassment. If that sounds like a Hidden Acting Agenda, it is. In reality, it's these same weird and secret thoughts that make a real, individual character.

Good actors blend these ingredients in order to fabricate a captivating character, just as a chef blends the pungent spices in a great curry.

"*The unexamined life is not worth living.*"
-*Socrates*

Impulse

To create any exciting dish, a chef must introduce one or more ingredients that will bring all the other ingredients to life. Many of the best chefs choose their special ingredient on impulse. This often comes from a notion such as: "I wonder what would happen if I added ...?" Taking a risk is one of the exciting aspects of creating anything, from a snack to a movie.

Actors should give characters distinctive qualities of thought and behavior that originate within themselves. These inner thoughts, also called subtext, reveal the characters' motivation. Characters, like people, often disclose themselves by doing or thinking something they shouldn't. "I shouldn't take that money, but I will," reveals the darker area of a person's character.

Breaking a rule can be invigorating because it's dangerous. This danger takes many forms, from leaping out of an airplane at 5,000 feet to jumping in with an original thought not contained in the script. The forbidden fruit is exciting.

The same is true with characters. In creating a character, you add or remove ingredients so that you can create something more stimulating, exciting and rewarding. Therefore, character work always evolves, and never resolves or completes.

The process of forming or defining a character is ongoing and always unfinished because, just as in life or in the kitchen, choices and people change. This means that the character develops and deepens as you add appropriate ingredients.

Each appropriate character ingredient enhances every other ingredient, as well as the overall presentation. It's vital for you to remember that stored somewhere in you are all the ingredients necessary to create a flavorful character.

Simply put, you need to bring together all of your personal eccentricities and quirks to fully realize your characters. As you create a character, consider those aspects of yourself that you don't like or that you deem inappropriate—these aspects are, in fact, the very ingredients needed to create a dynamic, polyphonic and stronger character.

Essential Ingredients

You can't create a potent character without the following indispensable elements: emotion, objective, past experiences and traits. I begin with emotion because it's the prime motivating factor in both acting and life.

Emotion

In his book, *The Art of Dramatic Writing*, Lajos Egri wrote: "Emotion, to be sure, is as necessary to a play as barking is to a dog."

As in life, characters are brimming with emotion. Therefore, understanding emotion and being able to include or omit this ingredient is vital in telling a story. Whether you have or have not studied emotion, this section should offer a new look at the subject.

Emotions are part of what make us human. Emotions help us cope and deal with situations, such as success, failure, attack or loss. Negative emotions aid in dealing with negative events. Likewise, positive emotions enhance positive events.

For example, a sound in the night incites fear and a child tenses and runs away, or a threatening presence outside a man's house ignites anger and he steels up against the threat. Emotions help you deal with events and make survival decisions.

Without emotions people would have to rely on intellectual analysis to decide a proper course of action. This analysis takes time. In situations where rapid reactions are vital, emotions force you to make an instant decision about dealing with the situation. Emotions have a purpose and function that is often more effective than pure logic.

One early classification of emotion comes from a Greek physician named Galen (circa 200 AD), who identified four human temperaments—the emotional, mental and physical traits of a person.

Galen's four temperaments are:

✦ Sanguine (*irritable, angered*)

✦ Choleric (*cheerful*)

✦ Melancholic (*gloomy, sad*)

✦ Phlegmatic (*unemotional, apathetic*)

Knowing these not only gives you a history into the early levels of emotion but these four temperaments may be enough to start creating an emotional character. (Notice that all four are strong words, not fuzzy words.)

As acting progressed through the years the acting techniques aimed at regulating emotion developed into two completely different techniques. One stresses the application of an external approach of indicating emotion. This approach consists of voice, speech and gesture, and is referred to as "nonrealistic acting." The other technique, emphasizing an actor's true emotions, is called "realistic acting."

Nonrealistic acting expresses the outward behavior that is the symptom of the inner emotions. For example, in a scene, a man loses his wallet and the actor shakes his fist in the air and frowns to convey his anger. Or, as a woman reads a letter, she drops it and holds her head in her hands to indicate sadness. These are predictable, "showy" actions.

With realistic acting, the actress would generate grief just as she would in reality, and the actor generates anger just as a man would if his wallet were stolen in a real life situation. To express this the actors would convey the character's sadness or anger by summoning their own sadness and anger. The actions may be more subtle, more true to life.

Along with the differences between realistic and nonrealistic acting, there has been a debate about whether actors should *feel* the emotion they are representing. Acting teachers and their students line up on either side of this issue.

One side of the "feel" versus "not feel" disagreement was stated by Denis Diderot, a French philosopher. In 1830, in an essay, *Paradox of Acting*, he wrote that, to move the audience, an actor must be unmoved, untouched. He maintained that actors should convey emotion without experiencing emotion. If actors experienced the emotions, and played from the heart, Diderot warned they would give unequal performances from night to night. Of course, he knew actors felt their emotions, but this didn't eliminate the need for an actor to develop a technique of portraying emotion without experiencing emotion. The opposing point of view is expressed by the Roman poet, Horace: "If you wish me to weep, you must first weep yourself."

Some actors have disagreed on the emotional approach for a long time. They don't want any variation added to the meaning of the words. They prefer to just pronounce the words correctly and not add emotions other than what's expressed by simply saying the words. I call this the "just say the words," approach.

These actors fully believe just saying the words will cause enough of an effect on the audience. This is true when reading a novel, short story or any written work, but not where an actor presents the story. Just saying the words could become presentational, indicating and non-realistic.

Some actors act only the implied meanings of the words in a script. Other actors recreate the meanings of those words in their own terms, meaning that they use their own emotions to create the character. When actors turn to the non-realistic, presentational and non-feeling style, it's often because the naturalistic or realistic approach fails them or is too unpleasant to experience. Emotions themselves can be a stumbling block to acquiring the realistic approach but they need not be.

There are times when the non-realistic approach is effective. Even pretending an emotion can activate that emotion in our minds, lending credibility to a performance based on the non-realistic approach. The non-realistic approach can have as strong an effect on an audience as that of the realistic approach, if the outward behavior is convincing and done with commitment. Therefore, both styles are important for you to understand and develop.

Whether implied or actual, real or feigned, genuine or simulated, you must learn about emotions to be a good actor. This handbook will help you discover and release any learned or enforced inhibition you feel toward your emotions.

As you work your way through The Actor's Menu you will gain the knowledge to present emotion in a scene using either approach.

Ultimately, whether you, as an actor, feel the emotion or not is not the issue. The issue is whether the audience feels and is it affected by the story being told.

Emotion As Opposed To Feeling

The words *emotion* and *feeling* are often used in place of each other. This misuse can result in omitted or ineffective emotional ingredients, not to mention lack of specific expression. Misunderstanding an emotion can be as distasteful to an audience as going to a Japanese restaurant for the first time and mistaking wasabi for green tea ice cream.

The word "emotion" has two parts:

✦ The first is the letter "e" meaning: out or away from.

✦ The second part, "motion," means: changing position.

The word *emotion* is the offspring of the root of the word, *meu (to push away.)* It comes from the French word *emover (move out, remove, agitate.)* The American Dictionary of the English Language (1898) defined emotion as: moving of the feelings. The American Heritage dictionary (1990) defined emotion as: agitation of passions. The word emotion, therefore, conveys the idea that an emotion is stirred up and moved away. However, emotions do not actually travel or move anywhere, especially from one person to another. What does move is energy or vibrations.

Emotional energy generates vibrations which do travel. When emotions are stirred, vibrations are created and the emotion resonates in another person. This energy or vibration can be likened to the carrier wave from a radio station that "carries" the actual sound. It is your energy that carries to another person. It is at this point that emotions in the other person start to resonate.

This effect can be explained using tuning forks. One is struck, causing it to vibrate, and as it is held close to a second tuning fork, the second fork begins to vibrate. This occurs because vibrations from the first fork cause a sympathetic vibration in the second fork. The second fork "feels" the vibrations from the first fork.

Everything is "tuned" to a pitch or a quality on a scale. However, this reaction requires that both tuning forks or objects be set at the same level or frequency of vibration.

We humans are similarly "tuned" in that when affected we will feel or be moved. Only each person is tuned to many levels of vibrations. That's why a movie may touch one person at one level differently than another person. Overall, this phenomenon is why emotion might appear to "move" from person to person. Emotions, when matched, cause a sympathetic reaction.

A story in a movie or on the news touches us because we innately possess those emotional pitches or frequencies. Every person possesses matching emotions.

> "*Emotions determine the quality of our lives. They occur in every relationship we care about—the workplace, in our friendships, in dealings with family members, and in our most intimate relationships. They can save our lives, but they can also cause real damage. They may lead us to act in ways that we think are realistic and appropriate, but our emotions can also lead us to act in ways we regret terribly afterwards.*"
>
> *–Paul Ekman*

An emotion is subjective and personal to each person because the resonance results in an internal experience. This emotional experience is the unconscious, unplanned response to external events, such as watching someone crash into your car or being referred to by an epithet. The only thing that travels is energy and that energy causes a reaction in your emotions.

Feelings As Opposed To Emotion

Feelings are different than emotions. A feeling can be a subjective point of view, such as: "I feel this decision is not effective," or it can be an awareness about something, such as: "I feel it's going to rain," or it can be connected to a sensation, such as: "The room feels hot." Feelings can also be described as the memory of emotion. It is the impression without the emotion. (Please note for yourself that "feeling" has several meanings, while emotion has only one.)

There may be some situations where you feel heaviness, emptiness. You feel this way because you are resonating with an earlier time of grief, making you feel sad. But as an actor, you don't need to feel grief to show it. You need only to slump as if a weight is forcing you down, and without smiling, speak slowly and flatly. This is a nonrealistic way of showing grief, and your feelings are not required to carry it off.

Whether *feeling* is an awareness, a sensation or the result of emotion, there is one fact about feeling that you must know as an actor—it is not you who must feel, it is the audience. Actors don't have to feel or even perceive their emotions, but audiences must.

"The only measure of fine acting is what the character feels. It doesn't matter a damn if the actor does or does not feel. He can feel nothing or suffer the agonies of the damned but unless that is communicated to the guy who paid... to see it, then he's failed. The question is did the guy in the 10th row or the lady in the blue dress feel it? If they did, then you've been a total success."
–George C. Scott

What you feel is unimportant compared to what the audience feels. Actors often believe that because *they* can "feel their emotion" the audience is experiencing that emotion, which is not necessarily the case. As part of an audience, you can watch a self-centered actor "feel" an emotion, while you don't feel a thing.

Actors often misuse the word *feel* when they describe their performance: "I didn't feel the moment" and the most overused use, "I don't feel the audition (performance, rehearsal) went well." You can have a perception that the casting person did not like your audition, but because feelings come from some internal cause, that thought could either be coming from your Hidden Acting Agenda, or it could be that you are not prepared enough.

Without experience, the only way to be aware of your performance is to discover how you affect others. Do not rely on your "feelings." To repeat, actors do not have to feel, but the audience does.

Actors transmit, like a radio station. The audience receives like a radio. When you try to transmit to yourself, you get in your own way. It's like laughing at your own joke; an audience isn't needed.

You can't effectively receive and transmit at the same time. You can't be on the stage and in the audience at the same time.

I have actually heard actors, after auditioning for me, say to themselves out loud, "Wow, that was good. I really felt that." They were so caught up in receiving and then praising themselves on what they were doing that they didn't care about affecting me. A bad mistake.

People who are engrossed in what they are doing are not aware of feeling or transmitting. In the throes of a fight, a victory or a loss, you may have an idea of how you feel but will not be fully cognizant of it. Nor do you realize that you are causing an internal reaction in other people because of your complete involvement in your action.

When you are totally involved with transmitting or expressing a character's emotions, you often do not realize the depth or effect of your emotions until afterwards. During this you will of course feel something, but you will be unaware of the feeling. This can be called "being in the moment."

Experienced actors have learned how to be in the moment. They are aware of what they are doing and how they come across to an audience. Experience is a great teacher.

For evidence on how unreliable feelings can be, ask another actor: "How many auditions did you feel you lost, but actually booked?" Or, "How many auditions did you feel you "nailed" but didn't even get a callback?" The answers are often that they got the job when they thought they didn't, and they lost the job when they thought they had it. Feelings played no part in the outcome.

To reiterate, during a performance, you will feel emotions but that fact does not mean that you are affecting the audience. Learn to distinguish the difference between feeling and emotion. An actor's purpose is to express emotions that arouse like emotions in the audience. It's only important to express an emotion that stimulates emotions or feelings in others.

Perceptions

Actors have perceptions; some are true, others are not. Perception is knowing through the senses, such as sight. Perception is also "seeing" what can't be seen, usually without any sensation. Perception can mean obtaining information before it happens or is revealed, like knowing when the phone is about to ring or what someone is about to say.

Sometimes when a person says *feel* they are not talking about feelings, but expressing a perception. Right after an audition an actor can say to himself, "I feel he didn't like me." This can either mean that the actor perceived that the casting agent didn't like what he did or it may be an expression of low self-esteem. In either case the actor doesn't really "feel" anything.

Perceptions have their place, but as an actor, you don't want an audience to perceive what you are expressing. You want them to resonate, to feel, to experience it.

I Can Eat; Therefore, I Can Cook

Do not assume that because you have feelings or emotions, you can successfully cause an audience to resonate. This is like assuming that you can cook because you can eat.

You should work at presenting all emotions to discover whether or not you can affect an audience. How will you know? One way is to present a wide range of emotions to a group of people, such as an acting workshop, and get feedback. Find out it they "got it."

Assumptions blanket the experience of being an actor, as in, "I can cry; therefore, I can act." Or people may assume that, because their friends laugh at their stories, they are ready to become a stand-up comedian. These opinions may be true, but they need to be verified.

To rule out any assumption about your acting, put your work in front of an audience, attend an acting workshop or go to an audition. During auditions, professional casting agents do not make assumptions as to whether an actor is right for a role without evidence. They watch for the actor to demonstrate ability. Of course, physical characteristics sometimes can change the outcome of an audition, but if you affect the casting people, they may later remember you for another role.

I devised The Actor's Menu so you could prove, not assume, that your acting choices can affect an audience in the way you want. To accomplish that, you must verify whether what you assume about yourself is really the truth for others as well.

Distinguishing Emotions

In order for you to produce a strong effect on the audience, you not only have to differentiate feeling from emotions, but you must understand specific emotions and attitudes as well. Expressing emotionally multi-layered characters begins with connecting fully understood emotions to your personal experiences.

Being personal is important because the emotions an audience experiences should be as real as if they were personally experiencing an actual event. Emotional events in life are tangible, you feel them. Therefore, to be effective, your character must be as real as real life. For you, this starts with an actable, emotional word that excites an emotion.

> "*Some* of us are naturally more attuned to the emotional mind's special symbolic modes: metaphor, simile, along with poetry, song and fable, are all cast in the language of the heart. So too are the dreams and myths, in which loose associations determine the flow of the narrative, abiding by the logic of the emotional mind. Those who have a natural attunement to their own heart's voice—the language of emotion—are sure to be more adept at articulating its messages, whether as a novelist, songwriter or psychotherapist."
>
> *–Daniel Goleman, Ph.D.*

After you define emotions you must identify which emotions you can act and which you cannot act. Emotions, like feelings and attitudes, must be actable. If you can't act an emotion, try combining it with other emotions so you can. For example, unlike anger, which you can act, you cannot act "love." (See page 108.) To express love you would need to combine two or more ingredients or elements.

If an emotion is difficult for you, make sure you have defined it, and then check if it's actable. Also check to see if a Hidden Acting Agenda may be blocking that emotion. Once these steps are done, you can work that emotion into a scene.

Levels Of Emotions

There are degrees or shadings of emotions that when grouped together will help you make a choice of a specific emotion. All emotions should be included in your groupings, even those emotions you consider to be irrational, because no emotion is irrational if it is appropriate to the story.

The value of irrational emotions is that they lead you into areas that your rational, reason-controlled mind often blocks. When you are emotional the thoughts that occur during that time would not arise in calmer moments. Knowing and allowing these different levels of emotion will lead you to thoughts and ideas that can electrify a character and an audience.

When selecting emotions from a group, I use a 1 to 10 scale to arrange emotions that fall under the same heading. On an anger scale, "rage" would be a 10 and "annoyance" would be a 2. Many actors lump all anger emotions together and try to present the resulting hodgepodge in hopes that something will work. This, however, is less effective.

The idea of incremental scales for emotions is as important as measuring the amount of seasoning to be added to a marinara sauce. Some like the sauce spicy, others prefer it more mild. Presenting emotions means presenting a specific choice or level. For example, if anger is suitable to the story, don't select rage. "Rage" is defined as: uncontrolled anger. "Anger" is defined as: extreme hostility. These are levels and each presents a different impression. Rage, by definition, conveys more intensity, which results in a different and more intense action for your character.

Every level of emotion tells a different and specific story. Within the definition of an emotion, you might find another level of that emotion. Use the level of emotion that stirs the strongest impression on you, while making sure it is appropriate to the story.

The following definitions are not clinical in their completeness, by any means, but they can help clear up any general confusion about these emotions, attitudes and feelings. By reading through these you may gather an impression that will stimulate your desire to create these emotions in your work.

Emotions Up Close And Personal

This section contains the definitions of words that represent emotions, attitudes and actions. I have selected specific emotions as examples for each group. I am aware that you may already know some of what is to follow. But perhaps there is one piece of information that can enhance your acting menu, which is new to you or stated in a way you haven't heard before. There may be a definition or a thought about an emotion that will open up that particular emotion for you in a new way. That alone will make reading this section worth your while.

Your work in developing emotions begins with fully understanding the words that represent what is within you. Sometimes actors work off of incomplete definitions for emotions that otherwise would, if completely defined, generate dynamic actions. As Denis Diderot put it: "... words are no more and never can be more than symbols, indicating a thought, a feeling or an idea, symbols which need action, gesture, intonation, and a whole context of circumstances, to give them full significance."

I have arranged the selected emotions that follow in groups, from intense to less intense. I group emotions this way for two reasons: 1) it lays out a progression of specific emotions, 2) sometimes actors do not realize the variety of emotions and their effects that are available to them for use in creating a strong impression.

You will find there are more emotions than are mentioned here. It is up to you to discover them and use them to create your own groups. Write these into your journal and work with them in a workshop. This will help you to develop your levels of emotion.

You must determine if a particular emotion or attitude is actable as the emotion or attitude is defined. If you think an emotion is not actable for you, get it defined and try it out in a workshop. Some emotions and attitudes are actually not actable. Love is called an emotion, but as I have mentioned before, love is not actable.

Happiness

This first group of emotions is categorized under the general heading of Happiness. But if you were to place like emotions in order of their intensity, from top to bottom, happiness would not be at the top of the scale. Sometimes it's a close call as to which emotion is stronger. You can make that decision as you work with the emotions.

BLISS: extreme or supreme happiness.

EXHILARATION: happiness and excitement; intense high spirits.

EXCITEMENT: to be stimulated to activity. Excitement is pulse racing, thoughts in rapid fire, muscles ready for anything. Being excited is generally connected to happiness but by definition it connects to other emotions as well.

JOY: an extreme, rapturous pleasure. Joy is more intense than happiness, thus, higher on the scale.

ENTHUSIASM: intense interest or involvement.

GLEE: open delight; great happiness; a giddiness.

HAPPINESS: a pleasurable response to receiving something

pleasant and unexpected, to receiving something wanted or sought after. The expression of happiness is most often just a brief outburst or a brief experience.

INTEREST: to be engaged in, to excite the attention of, concerned. This doesn't mean you should tilt your head and stare at the other person. You need to have an inner excitement and a desire to become willingly engaged in the person or thing.

FLIRTATION: to amuse oneself in playful amorousness. I include this one to separate it from the maze of definitions in the love category. Flirting is done for the pleasure of the doer. It's the first, light approach to a relationship.

CONTENTMENT: satisfied; wanting no more.

Of this list, contentment is unactable.

SMILE: a physical manifestation usually linked to joy or happiness. I've included this because it explains why smiling without real intention isn't effective. A smile is not really an emotion or attitude but a strong indicator that often is unsuccessful and is so because the mechanics of an actual smile aren't understood.

Basically, smiles result from pleasure and displeasure. A smile results from joy or, in the hands of a confident actor, becomes a great mask to cover something not joyful. Some have a naturally good smile, others should work on it. Forced smiles in an audition point to fear and an actor who isn't going to deliver.

Dr. Paul Ekman identified more than 15 different smiles. He separates a smile of true enjoyment from a smile of non-enjoyment by the muscle orbiting the eye. This muscle only responds to the inner joy of a person, not to the will of a person.

> "*A*ctors who convincingly look as if they are enjoying themselves are either among that small group who can contract the outer part of this muscle (the muscle surrounding the eye socket) voluntarily, or, more likely they are retrieving a memory that generates the emotion, which then produces the true involuntary expression."
> –Dr. Paul Ekman

A smile, of course, is actable. But can you make it real? Can you find the inner joy that will make your orbital muscle express true happiness? If you can't, your smile will look insincere.

Anger

Warning:

Aggression in a scene is limited to only an actor's intention or thoughts toward another person. Because the action is physical, you shouldn't attempt it without the direction of a knowledgeable stunt coordinator. Don't ever play around with weapons of any kind. It is your intention that should scare or affect, not a weapon. In my classes, if you can't affect me with a paper knife or a paper gun, you are not doing your job.

Again, starting with the most intense.

RAGE: a violent anger. Rage is fierce action. Don't hold back from anger, but hold back from releasing rage. Once released, rage is hard to control. Rage causes people to get hurt and valuables destroyed.

AGGRESSION: attack, intent to harm. One of the Sanguine (see page 86) or anger behaviors. Aggression carries out the anger impulse, the intention to harm another. Think of what you will do to the other character and "see" that happen *on* them, not in your head. ("On them" means that you mentally picture the damage and you project that mental image onto their real face or body.)

ANGER: a forceful reaction in intent, voice and action. Anger is an impetus to protect, to avenge openly a wrong, an injustice or injury. Anger is coping with negative events. Anger can result from the pain of losing or potentially losing something in the immediate environment.

HOSTILITY: a strong antagonism. It's an emotion that contains a possible explosion. "This damned shirt doesn't fit" refers to the shirt as an enemy. It describes open warfare and the shirt may be destroyed.

ANTAGONISM: a threat, an opposition. "Don't or you'll be sorry." It's an expression of a conflict without any active reaction. It can be similar to a warning or the precursor to an attack: "Leave me alone or else." It's active friction. This is not action but the promise or threat of action.

HATE/HATRED: a concentrated loathing, revulsion, disgust. It's intense, internal dislike directed at a person or thing. The key word is intense: strong, fierce, vehement. Prejudice arises out of hatred. Bigotry is an intolerance, an inability to tolerate a person, group or thing detested. Hatred is inward, seething anger. Hatred is free from any influence by reason. Hatred is passion. It permeates a person.

SARCASM: to wound. The root of the word is: to tear (rend) the flesh. Sarcasm is meant to hurt. And, by the way, it's not less painful if followed by, "Just kidding," as in: "You're stupid! Just kidding." This is just a very weak attempt at covering over an intent to injure. Either the stupid part or the just kidding part expresses the true thought. Joined together, the phrase is sarcastic. Sarcasm is all about the intention behind the words: "You look wonderful" or "Glad to see you are so happy" can be drastically altered by an intention to tear the other person apart.

JEALOUSY: the thoughts, feelings and actions that follow a threat to a relationship, or resentment of another's luck or ability. This often arises out of envy. Your friend getting a big role before you do could cause a problem for the friendship. The jealous person is demeaned by another's action or success. Jealousy can be described as a stinging experience. A jealous person blames himself for his perceived failing and tries to demean the other person for succeeding. It's possessive, so it involves wanting what another has, or fear of losing what you already have. Jealousy can result in anger, grief, antagonism and more.

FRUSTRATION: to be stopped. To frustrate means to foil, defeat, thwart, checkmate. Actors who actually are annoyed or exasperated very often misuse this word. An example of misuse: in a workshop when the feedback reveals the acting wasn't affecting, some actors reply, "That is so frustrating!" It is usually a misuse of the word because the speaker is not stopped, but annoyed or momentarily halted. When you are truly frustrated, you either quit or stop. You might experience what is called frustration in a scene or in a moment if you do not get the response intended. However, this might just be a brief upset, not an ending. In this case, during a scene, notice the feeling, then scream, flail your arms, or even sing, to push past the temporary blockage.

ANNOYANCE: an irritation, a bother, exasperation, nuisance, a lower, milder step on the graduated anger scale. What one person would immediately attack, another person might find just annoying. Annoyance can be strong or mild. Annoyance doesn't require any direct action. Annoyance is an attitude that can also be expressed with a groan, a word, a phrase.

Fear

Under this general heading are various emotions and attitudes that can connect to fear.

HORROR: an intense terror, fear, loss of control all blended together. It's a revulsion or intense disgust towards a thought, action or person. Horror is high on the "fear" scale. When someone is horrified, no action will resolve the horror emotion until it subsides. It's a state that, although usually short in duration, overcomes most attempts to minimize the source. Horror is a mental and physical freezing.

FEAR: a foreboding, a premonition, usually of misfortune. Fear arises out of the idea of impending doom, a fixation on the threat. This emotion is usually unaffected by reason. "Relax, it's just the wind" may or may not calm someone fixated on the outside noise. The bigger the threat is to a person, the less effective logic is likely to be.

Fear, it is said, sours the taste of the meat of an animal who experienced fear just before it was killed. Fear is not just shaking or twitching. There are physical manifestations, but many are clichés. Fear is a weakening while tense. Fear is a type of chilling inner pain that one attempts to make go away, but can't. Eyes are fixed, not wide. (Wide eyes are cartoonish.) Turn all the lights off at night and listen for the movement outside and you'll find fear.

ANXIETY: an extreme worry complicated by an often opposing emotion. Anxiety is doubt about a planned action: internal, painful uneasiness. It's seen through nail biting, or sweating, among other behaviors. "If I help her prepare for the same audition I'm going on, she may get it instead of me. What do I do?" "Should I wear this blouse to the audition?"

EMBARRASSMENT: to become self-conscious and distressed. Embarrassment is an unsettled, worried state. It typically occurs around other people, when someone at work points out you're wearing slippers, for example. When someone makes a social mistake, or realizes that they have a fault or a weakness, an anxious state follows. "I am so embarrassed; I thought your wife was your mother!" Reactions to embarrassment include: rising pulse, blushing, tension, a forced grin or laugh, touching one's face or hair, or looking away.

WORRY: an idea, a thought that something bad may happen. Worry isn't fear; it's creating what-ifs that result in disaster. It's an uneasy feeling or a threat of what might occur. "I can't cry on cue and the director wants tears. I'm worried he's going to recast my part."

SHYNESS: a timid, bashful, longing to escape. Shyness is a blend of many factors: fear, quiet, awkwardness and discomfort. These ingredients are largely created internally. Shyness can cause rejection or sympathy in others. Levels of shyness can be so strong that, in some cases, it comes across as charming. A slight smile tries to mask the real feelings as a young man softly says, "Hi, I'm Tommy. Can I ask you to dance?"

Pain

PAIN: an extremely disagreeable physical or psychological experience resulting from damage or the threat of damage. Some can continue with life while in pain; others can't. Sometimes thoughts are painful, particularly if one has had a painful prior experience connected to the thought.

Some feel pain on behalf of others when another person describes a past harmful experience, such as having a tooth pulled, or forgetting their lines on stage and passing out. This empathy, as well as any pain, is clearly revealed on the face. However, to completely express pain, true inner suffering is necessary to back up the facial expression. Otherwise, it can come across as false.

There are degrees of pain:

SUFFERING: to endure or undergo persisting strong pain.

ACHE: a dull pain.

DISCOMFORT: mild pain

Grief

GRIEF: the mental distress that is connected to a loss or potential loss. Grief is all about loss. However, what is considered loss for one person may not be for another. The death of a friend may vary with the connection; one may welcome the change, while another will mourn. Grief may also occur when people feel they are losing a loved one, such as at a wedding.

Grief is a physical type of pain. It's an inner ache caused by the absence, or impending absence, of something loved. The differences in how grief is treated and expressed vary by culture, family, or even gender. Grief stirs other emotions in the people around the grieving person, such as: sympathy, loneliness, depression, guilt, anger or anxiety.

Tears welling up in the eyes indicate grief. Losses vary from person-to-person, so that in a scene when you think of a loss, it must be a loss to you. Want to feel sad? Think of something you've lost. Think of a loss, a photograph that made you sad, everything you can imagine to elicit some grief. It's a fact that thoughts of loss overwhelm all other thoughts. Grieving people are hard to console because they are looking at the worst-case scenario. Deep grief is not one thing but a combination of loss, resisting the loss and inability to control the loss.

SAD: a quiet, suffering dissatisfaction with life, a person, job. Sad signifies a failure. It's expressed with or without tears. Sorrow is a form of sadness. Sadness is more lingering than grief or unhappiness. (See **MOOD** page 110.) It is a deeper feeling.

It is said that once we have felt deeply sad, life is never really the same. Sadness manifests itself when muscles are set, the face is very pale, you are cold, or when you face a corner motionless, offering nothing. Sadness can also be caused by fatigue. Think of a loss or of losing something, and sadness follows.

SORROW: the mental pain of experiencing or anticipating loss or punishment. It's another form of grief. It is deep, like sadness.

GUILT: the awareness of doing something wrong and regretting the act. A "guilt trip," then, could be traveling through all the "should-have-done's" and other grief-based feelings. Guilt is a level of grief that occurs only after one realizes and admits, at least to oneself, that one has done wrong.

SHAME: a disgrace, dishonor. Shame seems like other emotions, but is different because it's an overall negative assessment. Shame is powerful and difficult for an actor to grasp. Its power comes from guilt, which runs deep, and follows an act that was harmful to another. If someone expresses: "I am so ashamed," they may or may not be disgraced; they may be trying to cover up not being ashamed at all. Shame, then, is like deep sadness. It's a realization of oneself that is almost impossible to comprehend. Shame isn't embarrassment, as shame is not as light and fleeting. Shame can alter a person's behavior if it is really experienced because, with the shame, a resolve to change some behavior can occur.

SYMPATHY: to empathize, identifying with another's feelings. The audience is in harmony with what the character is going through because they have experienced the same event. Since everyone has experienced emotions, the actions of a character, when truthfully presented, will resonate with the audience. The audience must care for or have empathy for characters, especially the hero/heroine. Sad, somber facial expressions, tender communication, careful actions whether real or indicated, will, to some degree, affect an audience.

HOPELESSNESS: **the inability to act on feelings and thoughts.**
Hopelessness is overwhelming despair as a result of seeing no
future and sensing that all hope is gone. Hopelessness is flavored
by grief. There are vague feelings, but no action to change
the condition. Persistence fights hopelessness. Action lessens
hopelessness; lack of action promotes it.

BOREDOM: **a low inspiration, letdown, dissatisfaction.**
Repetition, without a specific purpose, leads to boredom. A
bored person can appear to be sad, and might be to some small
degree. But any inspiration will break the boredom. Boredom is
included here because boredom is often mistaken for sadness.
Therefore, if boredom helps you access some sadness (or vice
versa) use it.

Grief and its offsprings are different from person to person and
from event to event. Overall, grief is short-lived in its intensity,
while sorrow and sadness are deeper and longer-lasting.

Grief exercise:

What can you do if you need to cry but don't feel sad?

One way is to think of something you've lost, something
or someone that was very important to you that died
or was taken away. Remember that favorite toy, your
beloved pet, an heirloom watch, a grandparent, that one
thing that was near and dear. Feel the feelings you had
when it was with you and think hard about not having it
anymore. If you let the thought of the loss overwhelm all
other thoughts, grief will come.

Another way is to sit down and slump your body, lower
your head, squeeze your eyes shut, put a big frown on
your face and say "boo hoo hoo" (yes, boo hoo hoo.) It
seems silly but if you say it over and over and make it
sound as close to real crying as you can, and then add
the intention to bring up grief, grief will come.

Unactable Emotions

Love

LOVE: a deep, tender feeling of affection or devotion. Love is not a specific, individual emotion, but is often thought of as an emotion. Love is many things expressed in many ways and is impossible to act by itself. You can't act love as such, since it is made up of many different elements. Act the ingredients of love and love will be communicated to the audience.

> *"Although the emotion of love, for instance that of a mother for her infant, is one of the strongest of which the mind is capable, it can hardly be said to have any proper or peculiar means of expression..."*
> **Darwin, British naturalist (1809–1882)**

Love is a label for a combination of things. "Tough love," for example, when viewed from a distance, is seen as anything but love. However, understanding the intention, the viewer can understand seemingly peculiar actions as evidence of love. Convey the elements of love and the audience will understand it is love.

> *"Both parental love and romantic love involve long-term commitments, intense attachments to the other person. Neither is itself an emotion."*
> **–Dr. Paul Ekman**

If you still think love is an emotion, try to act it. Ask someone to tell you what you are doing without telling them in advance that you're doing love. Then try to create the "emotion of love." Love is not actable. The only way to communicate love is with several other specific ingredients.

LUST: a purely sexual feeling, either acted upon or not. To many, lust is a motivating force. Lust motivates thoughts as well as actions. In the movie *The Graduate*, lust motivated a mother to have an affair with her daughter's boyfriend.

PASSION: a powerful, intense emotion, fervor, intense heat. Because of the intensity, passion is far easier to exclude than to command. To deny blending passion into your characters is to flinch from learning to control passion. Passion isn't a gesture or behavior; it is an internal action, an intense desire that rises from the nub of emotion. Passion is that endless enthusiasm that affects everyone around you.

DESIRE: a zeal for something or someone. Desire can't be acted. Desire is a driving force to obtain the object of that desire. Desire has a scale of intensity, like emotions. It can be determined by the actions and intentions of someone toward a person or goal. Pleasure is the reward for obtaining that which is desired. Things desired are usually things not already possessed. Intensely seek a goal and you will generate desire.

INFATUATION: a crush, a one-night stand, passion with no commitment. Infatuation is experiencing intimate feelings or thoughts without the physical intimacy. Infatuation is often brief, but passionate. Infatuation is hard to act. Tapping into the memory of a brief period of desire, with no strings attached, is an attitude that could positively enhance your work.

FEELING: a subjective, partly mental, partly physical reaction or response. Feelings are received. To feel is to experience. While feeling does involve thought, emotion can occur without initial thought. Feelings tend to be a memory of emotion. (Discussed in more depth on page 90)

"The advantage of emotions is that they lead us astray."

—Oscar Wilde

Emotional Associates

ATTITUDE: a learned or developed response to a given thing or situation. Attitude is not really an emotion but a companion to emotion. It's the underlying positive or negative predisposition and opinion to an event or situation.

Attitudes could be the result of a Hidden Acting Agenda. Attitudes are shaped by experience and emotion and are lasting viewpoints.

Behind an attitude are all the thoughts, ideas and details that prove or support it. Attitudes can be formed by one-event experiences, such as: food poisoning. This event can create attitudes that are hard to change.

Attitudes also are formed by false facts, hearsay and fantasy as much as they are by empirical experience. Attitudes change, and the change is usually dramatic, if only for the character who possesses the attitude. Attitude is defined or revealed by a character's thoughts and behavior.

AMBIVALENCE: two conflicting emotions. Two emotions vying for prominence, such as: "When she left for college she was both excited and sad. Excited because she would be on her own, sad as she was leaving her parents." Many people misdefine this word as indifferent, uncaring and, therefore, don't use this concept to good advantage. Ambivalence is two emotions struggling with each other, which is very powerful to watch. Many times, emotional execution demands a blend of two or more emotions. Ambivalence is a way to put an emotional double scoop onto the character's cone at one time. One event with two emotions equals a potent character who intrigues an audience.

MOOD: an enduring state of feeling, lasting longer than specific emotions. Mood is considered to be about nothing and everything, as opposed to emotions that are about something. Moods are known to endure for some time: "If you are in a bad mood, let's just cancel the party." Moods are difficult to mask or cover and can be hours long, or days long. Even the desire to mask requires too much effort. Moods can alter how someone sees other people and events. Moods are all consuming.

Surprise: a breaking or shattering of an expectation, being caught unprepared. Opening the door expecting to see your living room, but instead confronting an ocean, results in surprise. Surprise isn't just raising the eyebrows. Indicating surprise by facial mugging, such as raising the eyebrows, is unsuccessful for actors who don't know to create a sudden struggle with reality vs. anticipation. However, indicating surprise can be an attempt to mask or cover shock or irritation.

Nonetheless, surprise is the experience of having what is anticipated shattered by what actually occurs. You can see a person's disorientation and his or her effort to get back into control, after being surprised. Surprise is a loss of control, either real or imagined. Note the reaction of the birthday girl at the next surprise party—that is, if the party is really a surprise.

Note:

You can use many more words to convey emotions, feelings and attitudes. Look for them. Cherish them. Understanding the thought contained within the word will resonate with the emotion, feeling or attitude in you. Added to your intention to affect an audience, this will bring your characters to life. When fully understood, words can excite a strong impression, and that impression is the foundation for a strong, affecting performance.

"Is The Character's Emotion Mine Or Not?"

After reading the Appetizer section of this handbook, you have probably realized that, as an actor, you can only express a character using your own emotional ingredients. Since an actor's work is always personal, your own intimate emotions and feelings are what you draw from in order to create an affecting, emotional character. You can be so personal in your presentation that the intention behind the words you speak can cause a physical reaction in the audience members. This "spine tingling," chilling effect in an audience results from an actor revealing his or her innermost self.

You cannot think the character's thoughts. In fact, you can't think anyone's thoughts other than your own, because another person's inner thoughts are inaccessible to you. Emotions work the same way. You won't "get" the fictional character's emotion from reading the script. All you have are your own emotions that are stimulated by the script.

Emotions–Finding The Sweet Spot

The sweet spot on a bat, racket or golf club is the ideal place to hit the ball. It's the ideal spot that gives the most power and control. The emotional sweet spot for you is your level of personal emotion that will resonate with the audience. Emotional sweet spots are the appropriate or ideal levels of emotion that create a strong character story.

Finding that ideal level of emotion requires that you understand emotions. Once you understand them, test these emotions in front of an audience. From their response, you will determine if your choice of emotions has the power you thought it did.

There are two paths that take you to your emotional sweet spot. The direct path is "fully expressed emotion" and the other path is "indicated emotion." (See **INDICATE/INDICATING:** in glossary page 183.) Fully expressed emotions occur when actors hold nothing back. Fully expressed emotion is real, affecting, and will include physical actions. Tears flow; laughter is unbridled; anger is intimidating.

Indicated emotion is facial expressions and physical behaviors that indicate or point to an emotion but don't express that emotion. Therefore, indicated emotion is accomplished by using physical gestures, emotional symptoms and behaviors. Some actors, for example, cover their face and mimic the sounds and mannerisms of crying. There are times when you will want to indicate emotion. As I said earlier, this act of indicating can affect an audience to some degree. Either way, by indication or by full expression, the requisite is that the hearts and souls of the audience must be affected.

Actors often "feel" they are in the throes of an emotion, but in fact they are in their heads, only affecting themselves. These actors either don't know the definition of the emotion or don't understand their job is to affect the audience. For example, if you thought being sarcastic was to be flippant and then presented that, the effect would not be the same as if you had expressed the desire to skin the other person. (See Sarcasm page 101.)

The emotional sweet spot is the most affecting emotion that is always the appropriate level of emotion for the appropriate situation, whether intense or mild.

Here are some ways to find your emotional sweet spot:

1. Use your own emotional experiences.

Your own experiences are the most obvious places to find emotions to explore. Remembering a first-time experience can bring up emotions. Since emotions are automatic responses arising from previous experiences or beliefs, the right level requires some trust on the actor's part. For instance, if you had no previous experience or knowledge about some object, seeing that object would cause you to be only slightly interested, void of any strong emotion about it. On the other hand, let's say someone walks in pointing a gun. You likely would experience fear because of your understanding of what a gun can do. Whereas, for someone without prior experience or information, the weapon would not create the same reaction.

2. Use observation.

If you can't get an emotion based on experience, then use your observation of someone who has that emotion. If you never felt rage, for example, you might remember how someone acted who was full of rage.

3. Use your imagination. (See page 70.)

Your imagination is a mixing bowl for concocting emotional sweet spots. With it you can combine emotional ingredients to give an experience meaning and form. Passing an event either one you have or haven't experienced, through your imagination, allows you to combine emotions or levels of emotions to find the sweet spot of that event. .

4. Use physical actions.

Physical actions can bring about emotions. Example:

> Furiously shadowbox with the empty space in front of you. The harder you throw punches, the more an emotion will be generated.

> Forcefully throw cotton balls at the wall. If done with the intention to release anger, you will feel angry.

> Slump into a chair and writhe as if you are in pain. This action causes some level of grief and the sensation or the idea of pain.

5. Mimic someone else.

One way to get to emotions is by mimicking someone else. By mimicking someone, you connect with your own emotions and attitudes. You can only truly mimic the exterior actions of another person. That said, I have had success in my workshops helping actors get in touch with their emotions by requiring them to mimic an actor they have admired in a scene from a movie. This exercise is simply another way to get actors in touch with their own deep thoughts and emotions.

On the other hand, when an actor makes a habit of imitating or mimicking another actor in a performance, the audience only gets a dim version of a character. Some actors work like mad to present their rendition of an actor rendering a character. This copy results in a ghostlike, vague presentation that is a completely mental, impersonal presentation.

The purpose of acting like another actor is to bring out your ingredients. Otherwise, an actor trying to be someone else may be flinching from expressing him or herself. This flinch is the result of not trusting or understanding the power of his or her own emotions and feelings.

As you explore different ways to discover the sweet spots that best tell the character's emotional story, you will also be developing your Actor's Menu.

Controlling Emotion

For many, control means to stop. A parent who cannot take the loud, wild behavior of a child may say "control yourself!" but they mean "stop!" Control doesn't mean stop, it means regulate, adjust appropriately.

You may have problems expressing emotions, if in the past you were taught to stop or restrain your emotions. If you want to create interesting characters, don't restrain emotions. Encourage, liberate and control them. Every thermostat has a point, called a set point, where the heater or air conditioner comes on. This set point, of course, can be moved. You need to be able to adjust your emotional set points to allow emotions to come forth at a controlled level. Control should mean choosing the appropriate level of emotion to most effectively tell the story.

Presenting Emotion

Acting is about communicating or causing an emotion to resonate in others. Being emotional is important, but it's less important than *expressing* emotion, and expressing emotion becomes less effective if it doesn't resonate in the audience. This is your quest: discover how you can express emotion that resonates with an audience.

Breaking through the restricting Hidden Acting Agendas or emotional training to display emotions scares many actors. However, as the old proverb says, danger and delight grow on the same stalk. The danger of expressing emotions is accompanied by the delight of taking that risk. If the thought of not complying with the dictates of your Hidden Acting Agendas upsets and scares you, you have found a big acting problem. It's a problem that is obstructing your development as an actor and one you must face, if you want to grow.

Not every actor can cry, laugh or rage realistically on cue. However, when actors face and overcome their self-imposed regulations on emotion, the task of expressing and controlling emotions becomes much easier.

In my years of working with actors, I have found that any emotion can be effectively presented, especially if an actor understands that control isn't a bad word.

> *"...anyone can get angry—that is easy—or can give away money or spend it, but to do this with the right person, to the right extent, at the right time, with the right motive, and in the right way, that is not for everyone, nor is it easy..."*
> *–Aristotle*

It's okay to get upset or angry or generate any emotion you want prior to taking stage, but don't prepare and plan where emotions should occur. Know what the emotions are, how they feel, what causes them and then, in the moment, trust yourself to express them fully.

Interesting Or Interested

Actors who are "being interesting" are playfully hinting at an emotion. Actors who are "interested" are involved with the emotion. *Interested* means being in the moment.

Being interested promotes not only the outward behavior, but also the internal emotions, feelings or attitudes. Being interesting is an outward show, without the inward connections.

The intent of an interesting actor is to delight an audience without having to be involved. Being interesting is performing without any intention to affect an audience. Interesting is expressed by an actor who seems to be saying, "Look at me, I'm angry," not by an actor who is making others say, "His anger scares me."

Interested actors are engaged in what they are doing and as a result are very affecting. Being interesting is an intellectual approach. Being interested is a visceral approach. The visceral, internal or personal approach is most potent.

Actors who are interested in telling a character's story and their emotions are genuinely interesting to the audience.

If One Emotion Is Good— Two Are Better

An effective way to utilize emotions is to bring two or more emotions into play at the same time.

> "*C*haracter Note #1: *The character-centered script portrays character not as a static state of being but as a dynamic process of becoming which we will call the carnivalesque: in brief, the carnivalesque describes an ongoing, ever-changing state in which character is recognized as being made up of many 'voices' within us, each with its own history, needs, flavor, limitations, joys and rhythms.*"
>
> *–Andrew Horton*

A strong character is a carnival of many voices—some in harmony, some in disharmony—that make a fascinating character when combined. This carnivalesque is you.

Your many voices create a deep, layered character. It's best to start with one emotional ingredient, and then fearlessly add other emotions as you become carnivalesque. Your quest is not just to release one emotion, but two or three at the same time. To demonstrate this for yourself:

Take a committed action contrary to the emotion you're expressing, an action that reveals an emotion other than the one you're dealing with. Let's say it's happiness. While expressing happiness by laughing, begin to stamp your feet and wave your fist in the air. This contrary action will lead to a level of anger, while you are laughing. Or, if you feel sad, force a big smile on your face, sit up straight, hold your arms open wide; you will begin to feel happy but still have the sadness.

Emotions can suddenly change from happiness to grief and then from grief to anger. While this sudden shift might be scary at the office, it is golden on stage or in front of a camera. The switching of states, even ambivalent states, reveals a character's essence. Variation or combination of emotions helps you develop your emotional presentation. This double-dipping emotional approach more fully expresses a character and is more rewarding for an audience.

Taking Your Place At The Table

When executed effectively and fearlessly, emotions generate empathy for the character's plight. Emotions can take a person on a journey not governed by reason. In life, this gives rise to the caution: never make a decision when you're upset. In drama, characters are exciting when they act under the influence of emotion, without much reason.

The best way to include emotions or any other ingredient in telling a story is to try them out first. Experiment without trying to get it "right." Join an acting workshop where you are allowed to discover and experiment. The end of this discovery is confidence. I tell actors in my workshops that what they will gain from their discovery is knowing whether or not their emotional presentations are effective.

This knowledge results from the actors testing their choices to know for sure what works for them.

> "*Corn is ripened by heat...but the soul is ripened by sorrow, just as truly by joy, adversity and pain, oft more rapidly than by prosperity and success.*"
>
> *–Newell Dwight Hillis*

Emotions, The Audience and You

What's it like to be affected? You're at a party and you meet someone who really intrigues you, someone to whom you want to listen. The person speaks and you are moved, touched, stimulated. "Have you listened to her?" you say to a friend. "She's enthralling. I don't even agree with her, but she's fascinating, she's funny and I can't get enough of her!" Wouldn't you want an audience to leave with those thoughts after your performance?

Audiences, no matter how intelligent, lose their separate, objective, intellectual thoughts when their passions are aroused by an actor's performance. The audience will resonate with emotions true to life and true to the experience.

In turn, an audience disengages their interest in a character when the actions or reactions of the character, internal or external, don't live up to their expectations. Audiences anticipate or expect character reactions because they "know" how someone would feel in that situation. When the character's emotions fail to provoke feelings in the audience, the story and the character become false and the audience is knocked out of the story. The actor might just as well be performing to an empty house.

Why Not Take A Shortcut To Powerful Emotions?

Walking in the forest, a young man comes upon a butterfly cocoon. Inside, he sees the butterfly struggling to get out of a small hole. The man smiles, as he imagines the butterfly spreading its wings and flying off into the forest. Wanting to help the butterfly, the young man gently pulls away pieces of the cocoon. The butterfly then emerges easily. As the young man watches, the butterfly does not fly away, but falls to the ground and spends the rest of its life crawling around with shriveled wings.

There are no shortcuts to growth. You cannot help or speed up natural growth. Just as the butterfly needed to fight its way out of the cocoon to strengthen its wings, you as an actor need to struggle through every acting problem you can find to strengthen your skills.

Discover and develop your own emotions, no matter how you stimulate them. Those actors who want to develop their acting skills without any agitation and upset, are actors who want the ability without the work.

Objective

Most actors know what an objective is. It is what one character wants from another character. For example, "I want her to like me." "I want him to kiss me." To me, however, the commonly understood definition is not complete. The word "objective" in fact has become a fuzzy word for many actors because of an incomplete definition.

In my workshops I see actors not making the objective strong and personal enough to be really effective. This is because many actors fail to define their objective as an ardent, fiery, burning, passionate desire to achieve a particular end.

The missing question is: What is really wanted? Further, why does someone want the stated objective? The answer to both is: Because attaining the objective will do something for the person. For example, an actor wants to get a role because landing that role will satisfy something personal for the actor; it may give him or her a feeling of pride, validation, or even money.

Therefore, the conclusion to a completely worded objective is: Receiving the personal rewards that come after reaching the goal. Those rewards are personal because they satisfy the need that made the person go after the objective in the first place.

In the above example, if he kisses her, she will feel that she is desirable. That is the reward that motivates going after the objective because it is personal. People do things to be happy, to satisfy a need or to comply with a hidden agenda.

More On The Objective

Christopher Vogler, in his book, *The Writer's Journey: Mythic Structure for Storytellers and Screenwriters*, gives an enlightening example to help actors understand objectives.

Taken from the works of Joseph Campbell, the protagonist or hero gets the "Call To Adventure" and finally, after all the ups and downs and in-betweens, he or she "Returns with the Elixir." Something is brought back for the good of our hero or others or both. Returning with the elixir was their ambition or objective satisfied.

Vogler lays out the 12 stages of the Hero's Journey. "The Ordinary World" is the first stage.

> "The Ordinary World is the place the character was last or the day to day world prior to the call."

> "At heart, despite its infinite variety, the hero's story is always a journey... It may be an outward journey to an actual place... But there are as many stories that take the hero on an inward journey, one of the mind, the heart, the spirit."

> "A note about the term 'hero': as used here, the word, like 'doctor' or 'poet,' may refer to a woman or a man."

The second stage of the 12 is the "Call to Adventure."

> "The hero is presented with a problem, challenge, or adventure to undertake. Once presented with the Call to Adventure, she can no longer remain

in the comfort of the Ordinary World. The Call to Adventure establishes the stakes of the game and makes clear the hero's goal: to win the treasure or the lover, to get revenge or right a wrong, to achieve a dream, confront a challenge, or change a life."

The final stage is "Returning with the Elixir":

"The hero returns to the Ordinary World, but the journey is meaningless unless she brings back some Elixir, treasure, or lesson..."

The Elixir is a cure, a treasure or newfound knowledge that benefits a need of the character or other people.

The objective is established with the "Call to Adventure." The hero is presented with a challenge to take on. In acting when a character wants to attain something it's the beginning of the adventure to acquire the objective.

The objective is realized when the hero returns with the elixir, something that benefits the hero or others.

This elixir is the core of any adventurer, a deep personal need to be satisfied.

Characters must complete the adventure of going after an objective and returning with a prize, treasure or lesson. It's something personal that benefits the character.

"What Will An Objective Do For Me?"

The objective controls the character's reasons for behaving as they do. It is the force behind their behavior; similar to the way that objective is the force behind a character's actions and behaviors. There is no more motivating force than going after something that will have a personal effect on a person.

What actors often don't grasp is that an objective must be an unambiguous personal desire. Many people desire love. Others want fame and fortune. Whatever the desire, the basic goal is to achieve pleasure.

We all do things in order to feel good. As an actor starting out, knowing little, having fun, exploring, you go after acting without much hesitation. You are very much an artist because you criticize yourself very little. As you gain experience, you become more of a critic. You pull back your creative energies and become less and less the adventuresome actor. This is caused by losing the specific, personal objective that gave you the early, wide-eyed, "I can do this," adventurous approach. This loss can be regained by restating a strong objective.

In your acting, characters who desperately want something actively pursue that objective by doing whatever it takes to attain the goal. This active pursuit results in emotions, attitudes and behaviors. When wording an objective, you must include the propelling action of accomplishing or attempting to accomplish a need, because an objective is not just a dim thought.

A strong objective, one that feeds personal satisfaction is one weapon you can use to fight artistic decomposition. Realizing the sensation or satisfaction of attaining the objective can keep you out of the doldrums.

Wording The Objective For Maximum Result

When starting out on your acting adventure, you will have many objectives. These objectives will be both artistic and non-artistic. A non-artistic objective can be getting an agent. You might have incompletely worded this objective as: "My objective is to get an agent."

That wording is impersonal and doesn't state what you want or what need is to be satisfied. Even "I want this agent to sign and send me out" still lacks a clear-cut statement of the personal satisfaction, the personal reward.

A complete objective might be:

> **"I want this agent to sign me, so that I can feel that I am a real actor."**

The objective is always completed with personal gratification. The need to be gratified is the need to "feel that I am a real actor." Along with that come the bragging rights of success.

In formulating an objective you should also know what actions you will take to get that goal.

A wording that includes this action could be:

> **"I will be emotional, real, affecting and hold nothing back in my presentation, so that this agent will sign me, making me feel that I am a real actor. Then I can tell everyone I did it."**

If this wording seems labored, it is. It's an example to help you to understand what a complete objective should include. You must be specific, even if you're wordy.

You can word an objective in many ways to indicate rewards:

> **"I need your approval, so that I can feel important. I'll do whatever you want me to do, so that you will have to validate me."**

If that wording doesn't work for you, change it to:

> **"I'll do whatever you want me to do, so that you'll have to validate me because I need your approval, so that I can feel important."**

You must word the objective so that it motivates you and addresses your own personal needs.

> **"Without revealing I'm broke or feeling embarrassed, and so I don't feel like a loser, I will charmingly convince you to pay for my dinner."**

Or:

> **"I will convince you, using all my charm, to pay for my dinner without revealing that I'm broke and feeling embarrassed, so that I don't feel like a loser."**

Use powerful and significant words. These can be foreign words, personal family terms or gibberish, as long as they are potent to you and stimulate your actions. You can detail the specific actions by which you will compel, earn or influence. Remember: these sentences are for yourself alone.

Example:

> **"I will confuse you, so you'll act like my Uncle Joe."**

> (You know how your uncle Joe acts, so you'll know it when you see it.)

You will notice that verbs are employed freely when describing the actions taken that result in attaining the objective. Verbs are action. A Russian theatre and acting innovator, Stanislavski, said that an objective is always stated as a verb because it engenders outbursts of desires for the purpose of creative aspiration.

> **"I will be so charming that she will be forced to kiss me, which will make me very happy."**

> **"By insulting him, I will force him to feel awful and I'll be avenged."**

The actions you take to realize a desire are part of a specific objective. Detail the actions that lead to your desired result. It is these details that help excite further emotions or ideas.

> **"I'll take her to the restaurant she loves. There, I will focus my attention on her, joke, be relaxed, do whatever I can do, so that she'll want to kiss me, making me feel that I am desirable."**

Whether you include detailed actions or not, you should always word the objective as a desire, need or want. Use whatever word you choose, as long as you define it potently. Whatever the objective's wording is, what you expect to receive must be crystal clear.

The Benefits Of A Completely Worded Objective

A fully stated objective reveals a character's essence: the indispensable property of the person. The essence of a character is personal and since the character's essence is *your* essence, that is what is revealed. And it is this personal revelation that affects an audience.

Wording an objective with personal details will make the intention of the character so strong that the actions force other characters into revealing their deepest natures. An objective worded with specific personal details also forces you to bring to bear your strongest intention.

As an example, this objective opens up the possibilities of strong passion and emotion:

> **"I will invalidate him and put him down, to make him suffer and feel bad so I can feel avenged."**

Another plus for writing a completely worded objective is that passionate objectives help you concentrate on what you want to attain and on the other character during the scene. In addition, an objective to which you aspire keeps your attention off any of your own negative thoughts or doubts. Keep in mind, the objective must be appropriate to the script's story. The wording of the objective must enhance, not change, the story.

Your Need And The Objective

Your need and the character's objective are intertwined. No matter what the character's objective, your need motivates the character's action.

Earlier, I used an example of an actor's objective to get an agent. That objective, worded to include personal need, would be:

> **"I will get a great headshot, attach my properly prepared resume, dress to kill, create an impression that will make the agent have to sign me, giving me confidence."**

This objective would create a powerful personal need within you. Your own need can drive the character's objective.

We have all heard about a person or a team described as "not to be denied." That phrase implies that their need was so strong that they will achieve the objective no matter what stands in their way. Characters and actors must also "never be denied" in pursuit of their objective.

Your need to achieve in the face of great obstacles provides power for your character.

Conflicts: The Consequence Of Objectives

Drama cannot exist without conflict. Conflict reveals the scope of each character's objective. The interaction between these two elements moves the story forward. A character wants something and, sure enough, conflict arises. These two ingredients rely on each other.

The opposition in the conflict ranges from your inner, self-defeating voices to another person's raging opposition, and includes everything in-between.

Conflicts happen as the result of objectives. Once an objective is established, conflicts and obstacles begin to appear. They seem never to exist until after one starts a course of action. They exist in tandem with objectives. You can't have one without the other.

You can reveal a conflict by presenting an important idea or a personal thought to someone and observe whether it is accepted, or has any opposition or disagreement.

One person may see an obstacle as a deterrent, while another may see it as a challenge.

For an actor, conflicts are challenges that are necessary to the story and to the development of characters.

Audiences love characters who fight through conflicts to get a goal because that's how they want to see themselves: people who can overcome all obstacles.

Conflicts are either external or internal. External conflicts can be caused by toys on the stairs, an absent server in a restaurant, a car cutting you off in traffic. Internal conflicts can be caused by the little voice that criticizes your every act, the mirror that reflects only your worst side, or the nagging doubt which you face every day.

An actor's car runs out of gas on the way to an important audition. At that moment the actor determines whether he will succumb or find a way to get there. Actors who overcome obstacles are stronger actors. Therefore, characters who overcome obstacles are stronger characters.

Past Experiences

Vernon Sanders Law, pitcher for the Pittsburgh Pirates, stated: "Experience is a hard teacher because she gives the test first, the lesson afterwards." We often refer to our mistakes as a learning experience. Experience is active involvement and the knowledge gained from that involvement.

We all have past events that control us today, some more than others. Current situations are often the result of what has happened before, whether in times long forgotten, partially forgotten or well-remembered. Past incidents, with their attendant emotions, help make us who we are. They are also a source for much of life's flavor. This is as true for a fully-developed character in a scene, as it is for you personally. Create a past for your character; a plausible past that supports who your character needs to be for the story now. Ask:

What happened just before the scene?

What occurred just before the scene is an immediate stimulation of the character.

What happened earlier in the character's life?

What happened to the character earlier in life defines who that character is.

If you understand the power of past experiences, you can enrich your performance. Never regret and never back down because of your own past experiences—use them.

From Then To Now

> Dave, a timid man, is afraid to ask Lori, his co-worker, for a date.

If Dave were a character you were working on, you would create Dave's past, where he learned to behave as he does. This exploration would emerge from your imagination and, more specifically, your own past experiences. Your experiences would blend with your imagination to create a prior experience for Dave.

Dave's timidity, you imagine, comes from his early experiences of being kept "safe" from involvement with other people and by being taught that "all you need to know is in books." His timidity could also come from a time when *you* avoided contact with other people.

Part of concocting an intense character is allowing the hard events and lessons of your own past to become some of the character's ingredients. Your own past is a storehouse of spicy ingredients ready to be used to serve your character concoction.

Early experiences and their lingering effects are the source of what might be called "baggage," as in: "He has so much baggage, it's a wonder anyone will talk to him." This baggage describes the quirks, idiosyncrasies and behaviors that make someone stand out in life. In acting, baggage is the gold that, when panned, will enrich any character. It's the character's subtext. The lessons of the past help shape character. Beliefs, prejudices, opinions, tastes, etc., can become the deep-seated, psychological underpinnings of a character.

Decide what occurred in Dave's past that would motivate his actions today. These incidents form his subtext, beginning in childhood and continuing through his life. Use these past events to fuel Dave's behavior.

When developing past experiences, answer questions like:

✦ **What occurred to him as a young man to make him think this way?**

✦ **What experience in the family prompted him to act like this?**

✦ **What environmental influences created his behavior?**

✦ **What successes or failures led to his actions?**

Have you ever watched someone's reaction to some occurrence and thought, "Why are they acting like that? It's no big deal"? Lessons from their past experiences are now affecting their behavior. *Your* reaction to *their* behavior may well be founded on your own prior experiences. Don't let go of your reactions of your past or your reactions to others. Let them breathe and add life to the creation of your character.

Let the way you were raised be how the character was raised. For example, a child raised in an argumentative family might be more given to arguing than one raised in a family that doesn't argue. If you were that child, your character also would be prone to argue. Don't prevent your own influences from affecting you and your character, as they can become the character's influences.

To plumb the depth of past experiences, honest introspection is necessary. Contemplate or consider your own thoughts, ideas, and experiences without judgment. Use them while developing your character and let your own experience affect the audience.

What Just Happened?

Either a script will tell you what just happened before the scene or you will create an occurrence to motivate the beginning of the scene. For instance, a scene about a phone call where someone orders flowers is more interesting when you decide that call follows an argument.

I had one actor in workshop who, just before a scene, actually made a call to his ex-girlfriend. He knew that they would fight and that would motivate his action in the scene. As the scene started, he hung up and walked on stage to confront the other character in the scene. This call brought very palpable feelings, attitudes and emotions from his past to enrich him and his character. If you can manage something like this, go ahead. If not, let your imagination stimulate the emotions and passions, then allow your performance to give them voice.

Fill out the character with prior events from the script, or decide what happened just before the scene that gives the current action a vibrant flow of life. What the character experienced just before the scene thrusts the character into the current scene. Let your imagination go to work.

In the earlier example of Dave wanting to ask for a date, ask yourself: Did he just get off the phone with his mother who was browbeating him? Or did he just realize that he left the iron on at home?

It is up to you to create an interesting prior experience for your character in every scene.

Just don't rely on lists of details about a character's past, such as their education, their job, or the number of brothers they had. These details are all good to consider, but won't have a strong impact, if they are not made personal and mixed with your own points of view. Your experiences, good or bad, affect your character, if you allow them to flow into your work. Explore and review all those stored feelings. If this introspection is done without blame or regret, it will strengthen your character ingredients.

When Events Of The Past Meet Events Of The Present

Unfortunately, characters have no more idea than you do what's about to confront them, much less what these upcoming events will reveal in them. They cope by using what they know from past experiences.

Characters need to be tested. The human test is always whether they will meet and deal with what confronts them. When conflicts are encountered, characters, like people, rely on past lessons to get them through. The events of your past might seem to conflict with present events. Do not reject them because of this conflict; instead, include them as part of the character.

Daniel Goleman, in his book *Emotional Intelligence,* wrote: "People who have strong episodes of anger or depression can still feel a sense of well-being, if they have a countervailing set of equally joyous or happy times." For an actor, these two experiences could combine to make a strong, affecting character. (See AMBIVALENCE page 110.)

Past, Present And Change

Characters must change, even if in small and painful degrees. Change is both intriguing and necessary for a well-rounded character.

Greek philosophers taught that a catharsis or purification is needed to motivate change. Ideas formed in the past are solid and usually unchangeable points-of-view, except when a person experiences a true, deep realization which frees them from these ideas. When a character confronts and deals with a past idea thought to be unchangeable, that cathartic event can result in a behavioral change that strengthens the character.

Don't second-guess impulses, even it they seem to have no connection to anything. These visceral impulses spring from the ideas and quirks of the past.

Whatever you choose for your character must be true to the story.

Finally, as you go about exploring past events, you may arouse emotions associated with these events. Therefore, tapping into past experiences is another way to approach emotions.

When examining your past experiences, do so with resolve and don't flinch from events that are unpleasant to revisit. These may well provide ingredients that bring vibrant life to your characters.

Subtext

Subtext is the thought and feeling beneath the text. It's what the character actually thinks, as opposed to what the character says. Subtext is the connotative meaning of a word, rather than the denotative meaning. Subtext gives depth to the literal or denotative text. You can say, "I'm happy," and drastically alter the meaning by saying it with an underlying sadness. Subtext is what you really think but don't express.

Subtext is vital to a complete character. If the audience understands the subtext, you have done your job. For instance: The woman secretly loves the man, but yells at him to get out in a way that lets the audience see that she loves the man. The audience sees what the man does not and wants him to fight to stay. The audience is saying to themselves, "Can't you see she loves you, go to her." All that is said is "Get out!" but the audience gets it.

Inner Monologue

Another way of thinking about subtext is as an Inner Monologue, also known as interior monologue or inner dialogue. These are a character's inner conflicts or thoughts passing through the mind of the character. These words, ideas or thoughts occur at the pre-speech level and therefore are silent.

Actors have many inner monologues that while unspoken are often perceived by observers. At an audition, for example, inner thoughts are, "He's giving me the 'I hate you look,' but I don't care... Wait, I do care! I need this... What am I doing? Yes! No!" The effect of this disjointed inner or private monologue could be perceived as an actor being indifferent or scared. Therefore, these inner thoughts are often detectable because attention is paid to them as well as to what is being said. This gives the inner dialogue its power to affect.

Private monologues can lack order, connection or coherence. Don't try to understand inner monologues. An inner monologue has no syntax except, perhaps, in a novel where an extended passage conveys the character's thoughts.

Your inner thoughts may or may not be in order. Don't try to bring order to your disordered thoughts or to a character's inner thoughts. Inner monologues are the unspoken truth of what a person feels as well as thinks. Your inner thoughts will become the character's inner thoughts, and these will make your character more exciting, as well as more stimulating for you. Make sure you give your character this interior communication.

Traits

A trait is a distinctive feature or quality that stands out and distinguishes one person from another. Traits mark the particular way someone acts, behaves or thinks that is unique to that person. Think of features, characteristics, attributes, peculiarities, quirks, flaws and temperament.

Traits also can be seen in physical features, such as a twitch, a limp, a speech peculiarity. An attitude, mental or physical behaviors, actions or reactions: these are all traits.

Everyone has traits, revealed in the way they act or react. These actions may or may not undermine their intentions. Remember Dave from earlier? He is the timid man who wants to ask Lori, his co-worker, for a date but is afraid. This trait for Dave is an ingredient that makes the character more interesting.

It is up to you to create the traits for your character from either your own past experiences or from your imagination. As an example, if you are doing a scene that takes place on a cruise ship, you could have your character fight being seasick because you were once seasick. And if you were never seasick yourself, you have him be seasick just because it gives the character a physical behavior which is more interesting.

All character traits enhance a character. Traits are the little actions or behaviors that may reveal themselves at any time. A trait added to your character expands the one-level character to a multi-level character. When a character enters a room, he can just walk in or add an unusual reaction, such as a shudder, as if hearing something fearful, or a frown, as if smelling something strange. This action adds more life to the scene and the character reveals something new about his past.

Traits are also part of your character's physical life. Stanislavski advised actors to have dozens of physical tasks. These can be anything from a twitch to a nervous laugh, or constantly glancing around, or playing with a set of keys. Give your characters traits by giving them a physical task.

Behavior can result from a pleasant or unpleasant event but not from a neutral event.

Aristotle believed that character traits were the result of acting in a certain way until it becomes a habit. If a person is always careful around angry people, for instance, that behavior becomes a habit. This, then becomes a part of who they are and how they are perceived by others. Many traits are formed as children and carried into adulthood.

You have seen a dog who, when you approach, lowers its head and puts its tail between its legs. This behavior comes from the dog being abused. Other dogs may act violently when approached—different dogs have different traits. It's the same with characters. When you add a trait, it deepens and develops the character. When concocting your menu, choose the traits of the character. Traits are a stimulating character ingredient.

Flinching

Many actors are filled with strong intentions, but do not carry them out. From acting choices to promotional actions, the best plans are often abandoned. Deciding to play a scene or a moment in a scene doesn't mean you'll do it. You may flinch, or back down, instead.

During your development as an actor, you will be called upon to explore your own personal storehouse of ideas, attitudes and emotions. You will have to deal with your prior training and experience in these areas. As you explore, you may experience "flinching." Flinching, or backing down, is often the result of early training, prior experience or Hidden Acting Agendas.

Therefore, actors flinch, or back off, from presenting their own emotions because they are afraid of the effect the choice will cause. Actors flinch from emotion because they fear their presentation will be wrong or ineffective.

Along the way, as character conflicts are encountered, actors are forced to ask themselves, "Am I willing to go through this?" The answer to that question will or will not move the story ahead.

Two things happen when an actor flinches:

1. The actor backs away from some idea or action, such as a particular emotion.

2. The actor defaults or regresses into a "safe," unemotionally challenging mode of behavior avoiding any confrontation with the emotion.

For example, if an actor believes that anger shows weakness, he will back off anger and default into a forced smile and bland behavior in order to avoid any contact with anger.

While in the whirlwind of emotional life, a person is helpless to exert any control. In such a state it's impossible for logic or reason to influence the whirling force of emotion. Therefore, no flinching is possible. Actors who flinch are trying to protect themselves from falling into a whirlpool of emotion.

Until you have risked presenting emotions in spite of the powerful urge to back off, you won't know if you can affect an audience with emotion. The fact is, as you go about discovering ways to reveal and then present emotion, whether expressed or indicated, you will struggle. This struggle is between the "logic" behind not expressing an emotion and the visceral urge to express emotion.

This struggle is inherent in life and often created by those who fear emotion and its effects. This struggle is enforced by those who say, "There is no reason to get mad," "Count to ten and then say what you think." These comments are great advice for dealing with day-to-day life, but lousy advice for an actor wanting to affect an audience.

When you decide that emotions should be part of your Actor's Menu, take the risk and create an emotion, whether it's the full expression of the emotion or the indication of the emotion. Don't waffle. When actors shy away from their presentation of emotion, the audience members are forced to intellectually construct what should be felt. The audience is obliged to put together pieces of a puzzle the actor has created. "He's looking down and wiping his eyes. Oh, I get it, he's sad she left." Mentally reconstructing what was not received is emotionally unrewarding for an audience.

Also, because you flinch, you might believe you don't have what it takes. Before you set in stone any assumptions about your emotional competence, follow the steps in this handbook and find proof of what you can or cannot do.

No emotion or other acting choice is right or wrong and no emotion or choice is too personal. When it comes to emotion, never flinch or back down. Risk your emotions and reap the rewards.

Seasonings

S easonings enhance the flavor of food; your character seasonings enhance your acting menu.

Improvisation

Improvisation adds an exciting spice to any scene. In jazz, improvisation is considered an instant composition. Improvising jazz music requires that you know the notes, how to play them and where you are in the song, so you can rejoin the structure after improvising.

For an actor, a similar trio of requirements apply:

+ **know your ingredients and how you want to present them,**

+ **know the script story, and**

+ **know how to get back to that story after improvising.**

Learning how to improvise is a somewhat troublesome undertaking, since it's difficult learning how to instantly do some unplanned action. What you can plan, however, is to follow an impulse without hesitation. Just as in cooking, if the impulse hits, add what feels right. See what effect that improvisation causes. You can't plan to get an impulse but, should an impulse strike, you can be *willing* to leave where you are and improvise.

When you follow the structure of The Actor's Menu, you'll already be improvising to some degree by selecting ingredients at the start then fully performing them. To improvise, you have to let go of what you "should" do and do what you think is "right."

The practice of improvisation requires that you act on a sudden, spontaneous urge. Improvisation is the desire and delight of the adventurer. Adventurous actors leave the expected path and find a new or different way to tell a story. This departure is risky, challenging and, when fully committed to, very rewarding.

Why Actors Think They Can't Improvise

Fearing repetition of past mistakes or fearing anticipated mistakes impedes improvisation.

A mistake on a test in school means a lower grade. An error in judgment regarding the distance to the wall can cause an accident. Mistakes can be harmful in school, in business and when balancing your checkbook, but not in acting. In acting mistakes often produce the gold.

When you know that making mistakes is beneficial to developing your acting skill, a new mindset toward committing an error is created. Missteps become opportunities to explore. Improvisation requires suspending the idea of right and wrong, so that using a quirk becomes an experiment to admire and celebrate, not reject and regret. Don't be afraid to make a mistake.

The other major reason actors think they can't improvise is because of their Hidden Acting Agendas. These agendas prevent any exploration that conflicts with whatever is being hidden, derailing any attempts at improvising.

" *All* life is an experiment."

–*Ralph Waldo Emerson*

How Do I Plan To Do What I Don't Know I'm Going To Do?

No one can tell you how to improvise, only that you should improvise. Here's how it goes: an actor wants to learn to improvise and picks up some books, takes a class or hires a certain person to instruct him. He goes through the steps as prescribed by the teacher. These actions can be valuable; however, by following this path he often misses the most rewarding part of the acting experience—the actor's own completely valid investigation of what impulses may come forth.

A good way to explore acting improvisation is to take a scene, in a workshop or with other actors, memorize the words and perform it. And as ideas occur to you, carry them out. Study the story, the motivations of the character and then perform the scene again, this time paraphrasing the script or giving it your own words while telling the story. Ride on a stream of consciousness, a series of free association's.

This current of ideas is the random structure of thoughts without regard to reality, meaning, importance or logic. An example: "I am tired the burger is overcooked I love her the rain is wet." If you find yourself tensing in fear or apprehension, you've located an acting problem, perhaps a Hidden Acting Agenda. Once any agendas or sources for flinches are removed, your vision of the moment increases. You can't depend on your perception when it is filtered by Hidden Acting Agendas.

Again, the ever-present caveat: You must tell the story of the character as revealed by the script. If thoughts come to you, take them. If not, remember you do not have to think like or become the character. As a matter of fact, you couldn't do that even if you wanted to. You can't think another person's thoughts.

Improvising actors often surprise themselves with an impulsive action. This is to be expected. Impulsive action creates an incredibly powerful life for the character and the audience.

Improvisation is using what you already possess to deal with the moment. In jazz, great musicians play the notes that aren't in the score. For an actor that means playing the subtext, not playing the script. Good acting is to act what is not known, rather than what is known, while telling the story of the script.

Masking

Masking means: to cover or conceal. People mask some thought or feeling usually for their own protection. Masking spices up a character by creating another layer. By trying to actively conceal some negative or damaging thought, characters become multi-layered.

Masking is also called "creative hiding." It's called this because the person doing the masking tends to be creative in hiding the real thought or emotion.

An example of masking:

> **"I don't have to get the part, I just enjoy auditioning."**

It doesn't take a genius to see the sour grapes behind this masking. Insincerity is a form of masking, in life and in drama.

Some social masking:

> **"What a great outfit."**
> Masks **"For someone half your size."**

Some masking is a little more blatant: "You're stupid—just kidding." One of those two statements reflects how the speaker really feels, and one is likely the attempt to mask that thought.

In social settings most of us are aware of masking. The masking isn't totally successful in life or in acting. Audiences love to see behind the mask.

Masking And Physicality

Masking can also be carried out with physical actions. For example, a bartender rearranges bottles, masking the fact that he doesn't want to hear the customer tell another bad joke, or a woman pretends to deal with a broken fingernail to dodge talking to an harassing co-worker. The physicality is intended to cover up and steer clear of telling the annoying person "I'm not interested. Go away."

You may have experienced a person opposite you at lunch begin to drum the table with the utensils, they may have been masking boredom and the urge to tell you to shut up.

Masking In Acting

In acting, what is being masked is often the character's subtext. Masking enhances subtext.

```
INT. Restaurant

A young woman sits at a table. She checks
her watch, downs the rest of her wine. Her
face sours as she scans the room and then
stands up. A young man rushes up to the
table.
                    MAN
          I'm sorry I'm late.

A smile fills her face.


                    WOMAN
          No problem.
          Glad you're all right.
```

Of course it was a problem. She was mad, but masked it. Masking emotion creates the pauses. The masking creates the subtext.

However, this masking must not be completely successful if the subtext is to work its way to the surface. In life, as in acting, we can be deceived by not seeing through the mask. Masking in life is one thing. Masking in acting means you cover, but just enough so that what is being masked is somewhat apparent. This allows the audience to be involved because an audience knows that people mask. It lets them look for clues that reveal what's really going on.

This involvement is like playing a game with the audience. The game of masking is played in two ways: either you completely mask or partially mask. In the first, no one suspects anything and you can build to a revelation later on. In the second, you allow some or all of the actual intent to come through. For example, if you were masking anger, you would allow a look, gesture or attitude to sneak through. You would let through just enough so that the audience would be in on, or at least suspect, what was going on. Audiences love to play detective.

Sometimes all it takes is a fleeting thought or feeling to stimulate ideas in the audience. The only exception is when the story demands the audience be completely hoodwinked, until the truth is revealed later in the script. This can be effective, if the audience is allowed to draw a conclusion that is shattered later, providing a visceral reaction. Audiences love to be surprised.

A very important step in your work is deciding what and how much of any ingredient should be revealed. When a chef prepares a recipe, he decides if any one ingredient should stand out or should remain in the background. You must do the same.

Masking In Casting

Actors usually try to mask fear, lack of preparation or any negative attitude at an audition. If fear takes you over, let the energy from the fear help tell the story. Trust that what you call nerves is adrenaline and let it go; the result might be booking a job. Letting the emotion out rather than masking it lends interest to a character, and interesting characters get cast. Do not mask your own real feelings when you audition. Instead, let them flavor the character.

Be yourself. Know what you want to do and do it. Once again, the place to try masking is in an acting class. Discover *before* you audition how you come across when you mask.

Moments And Transitions—Getting From Here To There

A moment is the smallest portion of time in which an action can be made. Within a moment, there is either an internal or external change, adjustment or alteration.

A moment is a point in the story where the plot moves ahead. During this point an evaluation of events or a decision is made. Moments can be a transition, a change in direction or even a thought (if that thought is made visible.) It's also a reminder to take some time to get out of the script and your "critical head," into the real moment.

To some degree you can plan where moments occur. Moments occur just before emotion erupts, during changes of the emotion and just after it subsides. Moments occur with new thoughts. And moments occur with changes during the scene.

An example: Jimmy approaches Sally in a bar. Jimmy asks, "How about I buy you a drink?" Sally smiles sensually and replies, "I would like that very much." Jimmy stares, a half-smile fixed on his face. Jimmy has a moment as he tries to grasp if he really heard what he thought he heard. He is silent, he tilts his head and an uncertain smile appears on his face. The audience takes in his behavior and realizes that Jimmy is shocked because he's not used to women actually saying yes.

Nature does not jump ahead. Nature is moment-to-moment. Characters don't jump ahead either, they move from moment to moment. A moment is created from the moment before. Everything in acting must flow. Actions should not jump from one moment to another without connecting moments. Sudden jumps in a scene, when not planned to shock the audience, will pull the audience out of the story and disconnect them from involvement with the character and the story. This doesn't mean you can't have a sudden shift of emotion and still make it believable. For example, you get a scene and in it your character must quickly go from intense anger to happiness. You may say to yourself, "How can I possibly play this and make it real?" Well you can, just remember that time when you were in the middle of a huge fight and the phone rang. I bet you had a sudden but believable shift in emotion. This transition is still moment-to-moment.

Good actors allow their characters to have moments of self-evaluation, where internal questions are posed and answered. These moments reveal the character, intensify the story, and give the audience a more affecting performance.

Moments To Remember

It is easy to remember moments of praise and applause when things go well. These times contain the best lessons for an actor. But other moments that need to be remembered are those moments when you flinch, back down, change your mind, and don't carry out what you planned.

These darker moments happen when your lines go up, when you panic, when you freeze. It's when your confidence disappears as you face a frowning casting director. It's anytime you don't give your presentation your all. These moments can become habits and can block your acting career. Steeling up is not the answer. During a performance, if you know when an uncomfortable moment is coming up, face it head on, don't avoid it. Remembering these darker moments allows you to discover how to deal with them and whether there is a Hidden Acting Agenda lurking nearby.

Performances are made up of moments; therefore, if you should become panicked in an audition or performance, deal with the panic as the character while in the scene; who's to say the character wouldn't panic? If you face these moments, you will instantly bring your own vulnerability to the character and to your performance. You will discover a lot about yourself through these moments. When good actors' lines go up or they get intimidated, they deal with the experience, moment-to-moment. They move ahead.

Actors who don't take each moment as it comes, jump to another moment of emotion or attitude. As in real life, characters shouldn't jump ahead. If you skip one moment, the flow of the chain of action is broken. Good actors notice what is happening and, if necessary, create a transition to deal with the occurrence and return to the flow of the script.

Your Acting Recipe

It's now time to combine all your ingredients to reinvent the character. This is where the real fun begins.

A recipe in a cookbook is a list of ingredients and quantities that are combined to create a specific dish. It's when the ingredients are combined that the fun of reinvention takes over as not every person follows the recipe exactly. The same is true with you as you create your character.

First, you will begin with your impression from the script. This impression or influence stimulates your feelings, images and actions. With these images in mind, you start to create your character. When reading a novel you open yourself to receiving impressions of the characters, the settings and the story. Reading a script is actually the same, with one exception, where actors are concerned: Actors are apt to bury their impressions with thoughts of "How do I do this?" Actors incorrectly read the script to "figure out" what to do instead of reading to perceive an impression. This impression, whether a first impression or a developed impression, is what sustains your performance and prevents you from losing the character.

After you get an impression from the script, it is time to blend in your ingredients, just as a master chef does in a well-stocked kitchen. You'll create magic for the audience as chefs do for their diners. The ingredients you will blend in are: Objectives, Emotions, Attitudes, Past Experiences, Traits and Moments. To complete your reinvention, you will fold in: Imagination, Improvisation, Inner Monologues and Masking. Effective use of the ingredients you possess will convince an audience your creation is real. As British art critic and historian, E.H. Gombrich put it, "Anyone who can handle a needle convincingly can make us see a thread which is not there."

> ## Before You Proceed:
>
> Do not doubt or second guess yourself. These are unproductive paths to creating a convincing character. A unproductive path goes like this: have an idea, think about it, find fault with it, dismiss it, think up a variation to make the idea fault-free, but the changes made to the original idea don't generate the same feeling you first had, so you give up on the whole thing.
>
> Follow through on your ideas and choices so that you can measure their effectiveness on your audience from their feedback.

Read The Script For Impressions

Some actors read a script over and over, hoping the script will tell them what's going on and what they should do. This is a non-involved, non-creative reading process. Read to discover impressions.

Stanislavski asserts that if a role doesn't leave an impression on an actor, that actor will be left to agree with the impressions of others. Actors who work off another's concept without an impression of their own present weak and unappealing work.

Here is an exercise that will test your impression-gathering process as you read a script. You will need paper and pencil.

> Find a new scene or short monologue and read it. However, stop whenever you have a thought—any thought at all. The thought can be about the script or the waters off the coast of Crete. Write down each thought, idea, feeling, reaction or

impression as it occurs. Then stop reading, and write down any more thoughts, such as, "I wonder if I left the stove on? I don't know how to do this. What did he mean last night? I hate this script. Why am I doing this exercise?' Write everything down. Now look at what you've written. Do you have many irrelevant thoughts? If so, this may be why you have difficulty receiving impressions from a script.

" *The* eyes do not see what the mind does not want to see"

–Hindi Proverb

To create a powerful character that serves the script in every way you must first arouse your desire. If one reading does not stoke your fires, the phrase, "the third time's the charm" applies here.

Approach each subsequent read as if it were the first read. Each time you read the script, write down your thoughts and ideas as they occur. It's from these thoughts that you formulate a story and enhance your impression of the character. These impressions become the basis for creating your character.

Gaining an impression from a script:

✦ **As you read for the first time, write down your impressions.**

   Describe your feelings.

✦ **You can also create an impression with a song.**

   A melody or song might come into your thoughts. If so, play, sing (or at least hum) the song. This can help bring the image or impression into focus.

After you have completed the first read-through, review your notes and delete any that are counterproductive. Anything totally off the subject, such as the forgotten iron or worrying about whether your agent likes you, must go. Save the impressions and thoughts that relate to you and the character.

Notice what images or impressions are created and detail them with words or symbols — whatever moves you.

✦ Now, read the script a second time, again taking down each and every thought or idea.

When finished, delete what is inappropriate and highlight impressions and images. If, during this process, you become stimulated, captivated or overcome with any impression, use this to begin creating your character.

✦ Continue this process until an impression is clear and accessible.

What To Do If You Still Can't Get An Impression

If you don't get a strong impression after reading the script several times through, try this. Find a photograph of a person whose image affects you. Scour magazines or photographic books for pictures of people caught dealing with life; they should not be posing for the camera. Don't use family photos or those from magazines or newspapers unless you're positive they're not posed. If you have chosen a picture that really touches you, it will stimulate your ingredients. (See page 161.)

Being affected is where you begin. Develop a vulnerability to any and all impressions.

"There is a vitality, a life force, a quickening that is translated through you into action, and because there is only one of you in all time, this expression is unique. And if you block it, it will never exist through any other medium and be lost. The world will not have it. It is not your business to determine how good it is, not how valuable it is, not how it compares with other expressions. It is your business to keep it yours clearly and directly, to keep the channel open. You do not even have to believe in yourself or your work. You have to keep yourself open and aware directly to the urges that motivate you. Keep the channel open ... "

—*Martha Graham*

Keeping a channel opens means omitting nothing. Keeping the channel open means not editing or preventing what arouses you. Your imagination must have an open channel, free from obstructed judgments, evaluations or logic. Keep the channel open.

After reading the script several times, using the affecting impression from the picture you have chosen, you should have an impression you can use to reinvent the character. Let your free-flowing imagination work with the impression.

Here's an example.

> Dave, a 30-something man, works in an office of cubicles where he and his fellow compartmentalized wage earners provide their services. Dave is captivated by one young woman, Lori, who seems unaffected by the confinement of the small offices. She is, most importantly to Dave, pretty. Dave, we discover from the script, is in love and wants to talk to her. He writes and records memos to himself of his desire to ask her on a date. He tries to carry out his desire, but chickens out every time.

The summary reveals Dave's attitudes, emotions and feelings. But without an impression to stimulate your own attitudes, emotions and feelings, it is hard to fully create Dave's. Many unsuccessful actors read character descriptions and try to act those without any impression or feeling. This often results in a bland performance.

If the above description doesn't cause an impression, find a photograph that makes a strong impression on you of what you think Dave or Lori would be like.

When you have an impression, get out your acting mixing bowl, take the ideas and feelings that are stirred up and create this character. When performing a scene, actors in my classes often find it easier to keep a character alive through an impression than with mere words or concepts.

Activating Your Impressions

Before you start combining your ingredients, such as emotion or traits motivated by the impression, here's something to consider. Actors often ask, "If I were that character, what would I do and what would I be like?" Worded like this, this question could lead to intellectual choices instead of visceral choices. This is because many people don't define themselves viscerally. Instead, people define themselves intellectually. As a result, actors have the habit of intellectually "thinking up" how they should "be" that character. This question does not serve the impressions true to the character.

Intellectually constructing a character or trying to be like another actor restricts impressions. For example, a famous artist was said to have advised developing artists that they should try to paint like someone else they admire. When these artists try, they discover they can't and make a mess of their painting. However, at the very moment they've completely messed it up, the artists become themselves. It's at the moment of confusion that a person's visceral nature is stimulated.

What this means to you as an actor is that you can try to "act" exactly like some other actor, but only if you intend to find that moment when you can't be them and must be yourself.

Acting must be personal. Acting must serve the character and the story. Serve means to measure up to, contribute to, gratify. An impression that makes a strong personal connection will automatically be personal to you. This personalization motivates, if not compels you, to do justice to that character. This is when you begin to serve the work.

An impression is the first step to getting into character. An impression touches your empathy and creates respect for the character. That respect electrifies the desire in you to prove yourself capable of meeting the requirements of the impression. Good actors serve or meet the requirements of the character, not their agendas or egos.

The best way to word the question is: If the character was me, what would I do, what would I be like? This forces you to examine your ingredients to tell the story.

Intellectual Vs. Visceral Choices

Impressions are personal and will lead you to visceral choices and away from intellectual choices. Intellectually you can "know" anything: "I'm great," "I can do what that character does." The challenge is activating your own ingredients to deal with the character and the story. Actors play a losing game with themselves when they try to "be like" a character.

Distinguishing between intellectual and visceral choices is important. Allow the expression and reinvention of the character to arise from your personal choices, not from uninspired intellectual choices. Ask yourself these questions:

> **"If that character had my qualities, what would the character do?"**

"If that character had my qualities, what would the
character be like?"

"If that character had my qualities, how would the
character behave?"

You get into character when you bring your individual
ingredients to the character.

In Character

Did you ever wonder what is meant by "being in character?"
Being in character is the result of connecting with your own
ingredients.

Look again at the definition of character: The qualities by which
a person is distinguished from others, nature's imprint, the
peculiar qualities of a person. Since another person's qualities,
imprint or peculiarities are inaccessible to you, you distinguish
your character with your own qualities. Therefore, when you are
"in character," it means you are presenting your own distinctive
elements or ingredients—your own qualities.

You hear actors talk about themselves and others as "being
in character" or "not being in character." You can easily tell if
others are "in character" because they affect you.

During a performance, you shouldn't be aware of whether you're
"in character" or not you should be too busy working with your
own ingredients.

Generating The Impression

If reading the script does not generate an impression, you can use other methods. Impressions can be fired up with a phrase, a drawing, music, a song or a photograph.

Phrase

A phrase for an actor in search of an impression doesn't need any syntax or proper structure. The word or words need not even make sense to anyone but you. They are words you use to express an impression or image to get you started creating your character. Impassioned words used in a phrase will develop your presentation of the character.

To construct this phrase, don't rewrite the story, which already is given in the script. Think of composing these words or word as a "designer phrase," a phrase designed by you, without regard for syntax or apparent meaning. Only the connotation of the words is vital, what they mean to you. Write this phrase to reflect your own impressions. With these words, one or more of the character's emotions, feelings or attitudes are revealed. The words you use should affect you, as did the original image, to assure that they indicate actable thoughts, feelings or attitudes.

For example, your phrase could be: "I hate people like him," "If love could kill," "Irresistible," "Chew-my-arm-off ugly," "Hottie," or "Bummer." Your phrase could also be a statement used by a person you know, such as "You can't take it with you" or "What goes up, must come down." The phrase you create should bring up an impression of the qualities of that person, stimulate your own feelings, emotions and attitudes, which can then be applied to a character.

Just as creating a recipe often starts with an impression of a past dinner: "I think I'll make that stew Jane served last month. It was so good!", the phrase you create from an impression, while not specific, is valid as a starting point. It touches your desire.

> ## A Point To Remember:
>
> A word is the skin of a thought. That thought is your impression. You can't act words, but you can use the thought or the impression to create your character.

If you don't yet get a strong impression from the phrase, do some introspection. If you still can't get an impression, try one of the following exercises.

A Drawing

You can even use a drawing to stimulate your impression. It can be a sketch that no one else would recognize but has meaning to you. Include symbols of any kind in your drawing.

Music And Songs

Music is very stimulating. Just watch someone listening to music on a headset. Music arouses, soothes and affects. Listening to a piece of music or song can bring up strong, connected feelings.

Music touches the memory as well as the imagination. Try playing a song or piece of music, get into your feelings and then, while the music plays, read the script and say the lines. Songs and music are a very effective way to stimulate emotions and impressions.

Photograph

Another way to obtain an impression or strengthen an impression you already have is to seek out an affecting photograph and go through the following photographic exercise.

> Find a photograph that stirs your feelings. It needs to be of a person involved in life and unaware of the camera. The photo must show the person from his or her head to at least the knees, with the face clearly visible. Then assume the exact pose of the person in the photograph. This means all of your body, not just your face. Create the feeling or attitude you get from the photo. Hold the pose and let any ideas and feelings come forth. Write down your thoughts, ideas, impressions.

The value of this photograph exercise is that, if it affects you, the impression is immediate. You don't need to study it intensely. A photo of a small suffering child has an instant effect on many people. The effect can vary to some degree, from person to person, but there is an effect. You can use this effect on your emotions, ideas and remembrances to build your character presentation.

Summing It Up

For an actor, each of the above methods, a drawing, music or photograph, also can be said to be the skin of a thought. Certain drawings, music or photographs seem to contain undeniable feelings. Each can help you create or enhance an impression.

Whatever method of expression you use, it must affect and motivate you. Whether your impression is expressed in words, drawings or symbols, it's your choice.

Start all acting presentations with a powerful impression. Get the audience's attention early and don't let go. Well begun, half done. Well begun for you, developing The Actor's Menu, means that you have cleaned out, or at least identified your Hidden Acting Agendas, have understood your ingredients and have created a vivid impression to send to the audience. Involved impressions will capture an audience's attention.

> "*C*ondense some daily experience into a glowing symbol, and an audience is electrified."
>
> **–Ralph Waldo Emerson**

Your job as an actor is to reveal to the audience how it feels to be in the character's shoes. Most good actors accomplish this by taking the character in the script and reinventing the character from their own point of view. The point of view of a good actor is always visceral. A good actor always has a strong impression from which to work.

You can use pet phrases, foreign words, epithets, photographs, music or poems—anything to get your passions in action. Remember what you use to get inspired; log everything in your journal. Since all your work is confidential, don't reveal it to others unless you want to.

The impression, phrase, song, poem, drawing or photograph helps get the character out of your head, so that you can work with it. Since we all love and prefer a story we can savor to a tasteless offering, this step starts your work with something desirable and satisfying to you.

Make sure your feelings, passions or ideas are stimulated before adding other ingredients.

Reinventing The Character's Story

The character you portray has already been invented in the script. And, since the qualities of that character are expressed in words, your job is to reinvent those qualities. Your character should not be a copy, but a reinvention from your visceral point of view. It is during this reinvention that you can expand and deepen the character's story with more incisive ingredients.

A Sequence For Your Reinvention

You can design a sequence in presenting your reinvention similar to crafting and presenting a meal. Here are some examples of a sequence:

Event → Feeling → Behavior

An event comes first, then feeling, then behavior.

Here's an example of this:

Threat → Danger → Fear → Run → Survive

And another threat example:

Threat → Challenge → Anger → Attack → Survive

A sequence of being faced with something unexpected:

Surprise → Reaction → Attempt to establish a logical reason → Orientation

It's important to understand the causal sequence and follow it in reinventing and presenting your character.

You can't have real affecting emotion, for example, if you don't have a cause for that emotion. The cause is what will fortify the emotion and make sustaining the emotion easier. You make a character act happy. But without the foundation of a personal cause for that happiness, the emotion can fade.

There is a cause that results in the subsequent series of events. And these follow one another. They, like nature, do not jump ahead. A seed one day isn't a tree the next.

Reinventing The Character's Story In One Expressively Worded Paragraph

By wording your impression into a paragraph, you can make sure you have included as many ingredients as possible. These include Objective, Prior Experiences, Masking, Moments and others.

Poignant words excite powerful ideas for your character portrayal. All affecting characters have committed points of view, they are not wishy-washy. As an actor brings a character to life with his or her own point of view, the character will become specific and detailed.

In the Past Experience section (page 130), I used an example of a timid man named Dave and the object of his desire, Lori. Following is their story in one paragraph, including strong words.

His objective is: to meet and take Lori, his coworker, on a date, which would accomplish his <u>fantasy</u>, making him feel <u>confident</u> and <u>desired</u>.

His Inner Monologue might occur at, before or after the moments.

The Masking would be of his excitement, his dizziness, his anger at himself.

The words in **bold** are actable. They are strong feelings/emotions that can be expressed or acted.

The underlined words are Dave's inner life, or subtext. These can't be acted, but can stimulate impressions.

The (M) indicates some possible moments or transitions.

(Masking) is when Dave is hiding.

(Prior Experience) is the result of past events.

(Trait) is just that.

(IM) is Dave's inner monologue or inner dialogue

> Dave, a **self-effacing** (Trait) (Prior Experience) man, is **excited** to meet and take Lori, his coworker, on a date, which would accomplish his fantasy, making him feel confident and desired. He **scrutinizes** Lori's every move around the office (M) (Masking), giving rise to unexpected passion in him that he must hide (M) (IM). Whenever she smiles at him, Dave **nervously** retreats (M) (IM) (Masking) (Prior Experience) (Trait), tranquilizing the **dizzying**, exciting craving that explodes in him (M). This retreat has always been followed by a period (M) of **angry** self-recrimination (IM). This afternoon, Lori asked Dave to stay late and help her prepare her quarterly report. Dave, (Masking) partially frozen with **fear** (M) (IM), **stutters out a hoarse "yes"** (M). Then, as they worked on the report, Dave slowly **relaxes** (M) (IM) as Lori admires his expertise. Dave frees up and asks Lori on a date, which she accepts (M). Dave experiences **bliss** for the first time (IM) (M).

Because the scriptwriter has already worked the story, your phrase or paragraph should be conspicuously about the character. Your job is to bring the character to life, affecting the audience.

Actually, the paragraph you write is the recipe and contains all the impressions and ingredients you need to present the expression of a vivid character. Further, as with all recipes, you can make additions, deletions or any changes you desire as you develop the character.

Now, one final step before signing off on your reinvention—ask yourself the following:

> ✦ **Did I get an impression from the photo, phrase or music?**
>
> ✦ **Does the phrase and the paragraph advance the visceral qualities of the character as written?**
>
> ✦ **Can I act the impression from the words I used to describe what the character is experiencing? (Note: not all words are actable.)**
>
> ✦ **Am I being true to the script and character in presenting the work?**

If you can answer these with a "yes," you're ready to present your work to a director, casting person or the audience. If not, read the script again and get or create an impression which will be true to the character in the script.

Presentation

In any fine dining establishment, the presentation is the beginning of the diner's enjoyment. Serving a filet of fish on a bed of al dente, multi-colored rice, garnished with variety of greens stimulates pleasure in the mind even before the first taste. It's the presentation that excites what is to follow.

Concerning verbal presentations, there are four traditional forms:

> **Narration: giving a detailed account, story.**
>
> **Description: to tell or depict.**
>
> **Argumentation: to persuade, present reasons why.**
>
> **Exposition: expose to view, lay open.**

Each form defines the message to follow. Actors must not confuse one style with another. Actors should expose the story, not narrate the story, as one would do in a novel. Novels narrate as they describe the story and the character's feelings; but acting requires revealing the character through the actor's emotions and feelings. Don't be the kind of actor that tries to tell or indicate the story without displaying the workings of the character.

Your outward presentation also aids in how your character is perceived at an audition, performance or workshop. This includes costume, makeup, physical mannerisms. Your intention along with your appearance affects the audience. Each element of your appearance must enhance the overall character.

Presentation also results from the inner-life of the character, and this is the most important part. An actor's preparation in this sense is the same for film as it is for stage. On stage or film, loss is loss, betrayal is betrayal, exaltation is exaltation, and telling a story is telling a story. How it's presented should only enhance the natural flow of the story. It is true that when filming, different levels of animation are necessary depending upon whether it is a close up or a long shot.

Actors prepare, develop and present their ideas for stage and screen through basically the same process.

Untrained actors default to "being interesting" (see Interested or Interesting, page 117) instead of maintaining strong interest in the story they tell with their chosen ingredients. When an actor flinches and then defaults into a superficial, mostly external presentation, it's either because of laziness or the fear of failing. Not being "interesting" but being *interested* is always the better way to present yourself as an actor at any time.

On the other hand, since people buy what you sell, if presented well, they might accept a surface presentation. Any method that interests an audience should be on your acting menu; just realize which presentation is most effective.

Claiming The Stage

When you claim an audience's attention, you are taking stage, demanding recognition and attention.

Claim doesn't mean to ask for permission or approval. To claim is to present an attitude like, "I'm going to astonish them." On set after set, when I inquired why someone was cast, I have heard people say, "Because they blew me away!"

"Blowing them away" results from confidence and from claiming your presentation. Certainty of your choices and knowing that risking failure is part of an actor's process are attitudes that have overpowering charm. Charm attracts. Confidence is being free from doubt. People who exhibit strong beliefs and have no fear of failure are often perceived as overbearing, but they make great characters and are usually great actors.

To claim for oneself is to "take stage." Actors who take stage attract attention to themselves. This is a confident actor. A strong presentation can force the other characters and the audience to experience their deepest thoughts. The true power of a strong, potent actor is the ability to evoke personal feelings in others.

At An Audition

Auditions can be intimidating and challenging. Questions and second-guessing abound afterwards: "Did I make the right choice?" "Am I what they want?" "I should have stood." "I looked down too much." The solution: Do your work; tell the story of the script, create an impression, reinvent the character with your qualities and then trust it and let it go! When the audition is over, leave all your thoughts, questions and concerns at the audition. So, as you drive away, you won't have to say, "Oh, I should have..."

Your presentation at an audition begins in the parking lot. By this I mean, get into your reinvented character before you enter the building, not as you step in front of the camera. Get into character well before you arrive in the audition room. Never wait until the casting person says, "Okay, let's read," to rev up. Enter with undeniable energy and intention.

Finally

Remember, you can take stage filled with confidence, but you are only halfway there. Nothing is locked in place, allowing you to now cruise along. Risk-taking must not stop. In fact, it must accelerate the presentation. Otherwise the energy and intention will be gone and you will present a stale imitation of what you have so nobly developed.

Dessert

The original meaning of the word dessert is to *clear the table.* This is done before the final course, the sweet that completes the dining experience. With The Actor's Menu, clearing the table means that you clear away all your planning, reinventing and associated thoughts in preparation for your final course—the audience's response.

Response Is Your Dessert

Obtain honest, useful responses to your work. Don't be swayed by directorial opinions or well-meaning but unfounded praise. Well-meaning but undeserved praise is like an empty-calorie dessert that fills you up but does nothing for you. With the honest feedback you get from affecting others, you can decide which of your choices/ingredients to develop, abandon or leave alone.

Unless you are performing to a room full of your peers who are known for their honest feedback, honest responses from which you can evaluate your choices are sometimes hard to come by. An audience may applaud whether they liked the performance or not. A casting agent may say "Nice job" but not like what you did. You may even run across an acting teacher who is afraid of hurting your feelings or losing you as a student and is far too complimentary in the critique. None of these responses will help you develop your acting menu.

There may be times when your performance elicits a response from one or more audience members. In a play I did there was one particular female cast member who after every performance had guys waiting for her at the stage door. She was receiving a response to her performance that let her know her provocative character was believable. I also received an unsolicited response. As I was leaving the theatre after a rather intense performance where I played a bad guy, a lady walked up to me and hit me with her purse and yelled, "You're bad!" It was surprising but proved to me that my character was working.

If you don't receive informative responses, ask for them. Of course, asking an audience is impractical if not impossible, but there may by a few audience members you can approach for feedback. Casting agents will usually give feedback through your agent. Of course the best response you could get at an audition is getting the job or the callback. And if your acting teacher doesn't tell you how you come across during the critique, then this would be a good time to ask.

Formulate specific questions that will get the answers that will help you discover acting problems and what you need to do to improve. For example, "Did I make you sad?" "Did the masking work?" "Did my emotion affect you?" "Was my character believable?" "My subtext was an angry person—did you feel afraid?" After the response to each of these questions, ask even more detailed questions to learn for sure how you came across.

If you receive unsolicited feedback, consider its usefulness; not all feedback may be workable for you. Beware of directorial feedback that isn't from a director; it could be damaging to you. Learn to ignore comments that start with "What I would do if I were you is....." You want to know how you affected the person or the class, not their idea on how you *should* have done it.

Don't avoid or be afraid of having your acting problems pointed out. Learn what they are and fix them, and your talent will flourish.

Inner Critic

Many actors insert their own, often self-destructive, inner critique into their process after they present their character and before the response. Without years of experience inner critiques are almost always misguided. It takes experience to know when you are being visceral in the moment. Without your inner critic getting in your way, you would be able to tell the difference between an audience who genuinely likes the performance and an audience who cheers and applauds while muttering, "I never thought it would end!" If actors take only the cheers without verification, they can make big mistakes in judging their effectiveness.

You can perceive another character, you can perceive the audience, you can perceive the temperature in the room, but you can't accurately perceive your own performance without experience.

Your perception and critique of your own work is a mental action and subject to all sorts of flawed conclusions. Remember that as an actor, you are the transmitter, not the receiver.

Did you ever trust an inner critique and later regret it? You may have said or thought, "I don't think they liked me, so I'll quit acting," only to discover they wanted you for a callback? Have you ever stamped a performance or an idea of yours as "No good," and given up on it, only later to find out it would have worked? Cherish any and all responses. Especially appreciate the feedback that indicates specifics which you can use to develop your menu. And keep even the vague, general, nonspecific comments to see if some truth or development might be gained from further examination. Within every falsehood, there is a truth.

Review

Now that you have received an audience's response, examine and verify that response in detail. Reviewing is not putting a "spin" on what you did; it is an unbiased inspection. For example, an actor might spin a response by explaining: "I *wanted* my performance to be void of emotion." Putting a "spin" about the lack of emotion doesn't change the fact that the character came across flat and uninteresting. And by not honestly reviewing the response, growth is hindered.

You've given your performance, the verdict has been handed down. Now you need to compare the verdict on how you came across with how you intended to come across. Rethink what you did and figure out if the response was in line with what you intended.

As you create and develop your Actor's Menu, you must select and combine ingredients that you feel best serve the impression you intend for the audience. You must examine and review in order to gauge if more or less of any one ingredient, or perhaps the concoction itself, needs to be reconstructed. Evaluating using a 1 to 10 scale will help you determine to what degree the audience was affected. If you discover from the audience, "Your anger was so-so," that tells you it may be a 4 or a 5 and you need to stoke up the anger.

Generally, any examination should be done immediately after the response. The review should also be carried out again later, when everything has calmed down. The results of your review tell you what occurred and how you might change your character recipe.

Again, for maximum effect, this review should be done without any judgment to right or wrong. Thoughts of right or wrong or negative self-criticism may indicate that you've hit a Hidden Acting Agenda. At this point you should investigate that agenda. Finally, after an audition you can do one very simple review: ask yourself, "Did I book the job, land the callback, or get strong positive feedback?" Too many actors base their review of their work on someone's comments, such as, "You were great!" This might mean you were great or it might have been said to get you out the door. Just because you hear words of praise doesn't mean you are being praised. The ultimate, flawless review is: Did you sign a contract? If not, develop your menu.

The Joy Of Developing

Actors often want to develop instantly and not allow all the character ingredients to join together to form a stronger character. Instant development applies to photographs and coffee, not Acting Menus. A good wine is one aged slowly.

"I want it now!" is the watchword of the many actors who avoid the process of developing. Development is the only process in which you should be interested, development that results in affecting audiences.

Developing a character is like marinating, allowing ingredients to blend together. In acting, you allow the ingredients to enhance each other.

Now, with the responses in hand, you begin to develop by isolating, ingredient-by-ingredient, what you need to keep, because it was effective, and what you need to develop more, if it didn't quite create the desired impression. Developing is building on what you already possess.

The true joy of developing as an actor is that it is a personal journey. Nothing should be left off The Actor's Menu. Anything that does not affect or work for an audience right now might work later, after more experience and more trial and error.

Less Isn't Always More

The "less is more" instruction is usually directed at actors who do too much indicating without enough subtext. Doing too much is also referred to as "over the top." That statement may be the truth, or it may be said because the speaker has limits on what he can handle.

If you were enraged in a scene where anger wasn't needed, it would be too much for the scene. On the other hand, if you express less anger because you *assume* it's too much (because of a Hidden Acting Agenda), you could be inhibiting yourself and the story. What you should do is work on masking the anger instead of diminishing it. Controlling, not lessening, is what I mean by "less is more."

The intensity of the ingredients you bring to bear in a scene, such as emotion, should either be let go or masked.

Lay yourself open and allow every aspect of an emotion, feeling or quirk to be released. Your natural process of masking can monitor the degrees. Learn to stop flinching from experiencing what may be challenging.

As you grow and develop as an actor, you will learn to trust your impulses and deep feelings, not limit them to intellectual value judgments.

Limiting, restricting and flinching is easier for most actors than exploring and releasing. Not disclosing your inner feelings, no matter the degree, generates what actors love to call frustration.

Deconstructing Frustration

Frustrate means to defeat, to foil, to make worthless, in other words, to stop. (See **FRUSTRATION** page 102.) Many actors in my workshops use the word *frustrated* when they didn't get the response they planned. However, they don't mean stopped, they mean irritated, upset or sad. You should learn to use words that mean what you intend. If you are really trying to develop, you cannot *be* frustrated. You can be annoyed and even angry, but not frustrated. Get the idea that to be frustrated is to be defeated, stopped, and only use that word if you are actually stopped.

Barriers and obstacles (acting problems) will spring up once you set an objective. Barriers are to be overcome. Developing as an actor will *always* be accompanied by obstacles. These are not reasons to stop. When a barrier has you believing you should stop acting, check to see if it's a Hidden Acting Agenda.

Development Is Natural

To develop means to bring out your capabilities and possibilities. Development is a natural element of the human adventure. Without the viewpoint of an adventurer, improvement is made more difficult, because risking, attempting and experimenting to discover for yourself is the winning attitude in developing a powerful acting menu. If you desire to be a more dynamic actor, be an adventurer.

You will be developing constantly until you hit on what is a resoundingly successful acting menu. A determined attitude along with persistence are affecting, powerful and the marks of a great actor.

Reinvent Once More

Now that you have developed the character review everything again. Then, if necessary, reinvent your character once again. Go through the same steps. Only this time, you have feedback to help you select ingredients. Each reinvention will fire up your creative juices.

"One of the strongest characteristics of genius is the power of lighting its own fire."

–John W. Foster

Learn to light your own fires with your character reinvention. Do this as many times as necessary to affect an audience. Reinventing is the joy of creating your Acting Menu, where nothing is wrong and nothing is ignored. Retain each and every reinvention in its original form for later review or to use again. Keep detailed notes in your journal. Too many actors have an idea that would work somewhere but, because of a critique (internal or external), they lose it, forget it or deny it.

Having trust in your reinvention is vital. Trust that creating a new, previously unimagined character will not mean the end of your career. Reinvention is demonstrated by recombining ingredients without any flinching or backing off. But first, clear the table. You must clear away any fixed ideas or thoughts you have after receiving feedback, before recombining and reinventing.

"Nothing in the world can take the place of persistence. Talent will not, nothing is more common than unsuccessful men with talent. Genius will not, unrewarded genius is almost a proverb. Education will not, the world is full of educated derelicts. Persistence and determination are omnipotent. The slogan 'press on' has solved and always will solve the problems of the human race."

–Calvin Coolidge

Your Acting Menu

Your Acting Menu is a categorized list of what you can offer. It's based on the Dessert section, which is where you received your responses and where you reviewed, developed, and reinvented your character ingredients all of which complete your Acting Menu. Your menu consists of what has been proven to affect an audience, whether it's in an audition, in an acting workshop, on stage or on a set.

Along with what you know is effective, your Acting Menu will contain both those ingredients in development and those you intend to test. Your Acting Menu is also a summation of all those feedback notes you put in your journal.

Your Acting Menu is comprised of:

✦ **Character ingredients that you know, with certainty, are effective.**

You can break these down by category, such as:

✦ **Emotions**

Which emotions were affecting?

Which need developing?

✦ **Masking**

Did the masking allow what was masked to come through?

✦ **Objective**

Was the objective personal enough?

Did the objective drive the character in the scene?

✦ Attitudes

> Which attitudes were affecting?
>
> Which need developing?
>
> What specific photographs move me?
>
> What costume and makeup helps me feel stronger?

✦ Hints on auditioning

✦ Info on acting

✦ Workshop/Classes

> What preparation resulted in the strongest response?
>
> What did I do that blew them away?
>
> What did I do that put them to sleep?
>
> Am I asking questions that elicit feedback?

Under Workshop/Classes, you would detail the ingredients you compiled for a character and set your planned presentation against the response, noting whether it was ineffective or not, and what changes you will make. (Remember to put these notes in your journal.)

✦ Auditions

> What character preparation resulted in the strongest response?
>
> What did I do that blew them away?
>
> What did I do that put them to sleep?
>
> When I entered, what was my personal presentation that did or did not grab them right away?

Any ingredient or character presentation that was not affecting is still in your Dessert section for development.

Finally, keep this in mind:

Emotions are fleeting at times and can be hard to capture, but they are often easier to get hold of if you record the impression you got, no matter the source. It's important to specify what you did, especially in a spur-of-the-moment action.

Continually look for photographs, music and real-life events that move you. These will keep your intention on the fact that you are serving a character by reinventing with what has touched you. Recording these in your journal allows you to refer back to them.

Costume, makeup and whatever external presentation you create should be noted for their effect.

Add or delete categories on your Acting Menu that either detail or fail to detail your acting and your career.

Achieving a captivating presentation may not always be easy. When the going gets tough, remember this:

"*Your pain is the breaking of the shell that encloses your understanding.*"
						–Kahlil Gibran

Your Acting Menu is the final chapter because it's where you celebrate your work and the feedback. It's the true dessert because now you confidently "clear the table" and lay out your most affecting presentations.

All my best to you and your developing acting career. I hope your process of discovery is risk-laden, unpredictable, challenging and uncomfortably introspective. And may it be a process that leads you, not to new places, but to gaining new perspectives.

Glossary

Some words in this glossary you may know and some you may not. Words have the power to stimulate images, emotions and actions.

ASSUME: To take as truth or fact without proof.

BOOK: To be contracted for a role, to get the gig, the job.

IMAGINE: To form a mental picture to oneself, to form an image of.

IMAGINATION: The power or faculty of the mind by which it conceives and forms ideas of things communicated to it by the organs of sense; the power to call up mental images. A synonym for imagination is *fancy*, n. contracted from *fantasy*: *to cause to appear, to imagine,* and from *to show, to appear, to shine.*

IMITATION: A copy presented as the original, to resemble. Acting is not imitating or making a copy, because one can only imitate the exterior actions of a character, not the interior actions. Imitating a character often results in obscuring and distorting that character.

IMPROVISATION: From the Latin words meaning *not foreseen.* Improvising is spontaneous—without an outside cause, unpremeditated, impulsive.

INDICATE/INDICATING: To have no intention behind an action. Indicating is a symptom, a token. Indicating is without depth of feeling or intent. For an actor, indicating is hinting at the character's story without emotion, intention or any real depth. Indicating is acting out the mannerisms of anger, grief or happiness without the energy of that emotion. Acting that is not indicated has a better effect on an audience. (There may be times when you need "indicating acting" so don't leave it off your acting menu. The real test is: if the audience is affected you've done your job.)

INNER CRITIC: That voice inside you that is always negative or at least sarcastic. If you listen to this voice without outside verification, you will be sabotaging your acting menu.

INTENTION: To fix your mind on a target, on what you plan to do. You take an action because of something you want to accomplish. Your intention is what you want to do. It is not necessarily what you want to get from the action (see Objective, page 121.) It is a stretching or bending of the mind towards something. "My intention is to book a movie." In that statement the mind is extended to getting that movie.

INTROSPECTION: To observe your thoughts, feelings and beliefs honestly and fearlessly and then to consider, without prejudice, what has been perceived.

MIMIC: Copying other people's voices, gestures, or appearance, often for comic effect. It is similar to imitating (see **IMITATION**) but has a sense of ridicule.

POINT OF VIEW: The position from which something is viewed. Your point of view is how you see an event or person. (You may see the person as sad, but another may see him as deep and intense.) It's someone's attitude or belief towards or concerning a situation or fact. Some actors see acting as fun, others as a struggle, as nonproductive and as a waste of time. It's only a point of view. Points of view are created out of experiences —good or bad.

A point of view can stimulate conflict or resolve a problem, but only if it's a firm point of view. All characters have points of view. In an audition too many actors try to perceive the point of view of the casting person instead of presenting their own. Practice trusting your own point of view. Present your strongest point of view in your work. Strong points of view make for strong characters.

> *"It is the eye which makes the horizon."*
> *–Ralph Waldo Emerson*

POLYPHONIC: A chorus of many voices. This is another way of saying levels of character.

QUIRK: A peculiarity or idiosyncrasy; an individual quality that defines a character. (Adding a quirk to a character gives it depth.)

REINVENT: To invent or create anew, knowing that in the case of a character, it has been invented in the script.

REPRESENTATION: A visual or tangible rendering of someone, a presentation of an image. It's similar to imitating and indicating. (Your agent is not you but represents you.)

RISK/RISK TAKING: The potential for loss, injury or harm. Risk taking is stimulating; it makes your pulse race because of the potential for failure. The prospect of winning and the desire for adventure creates the need to risk. Risking, for an actor, doesn't have the same consequences as driving home drunk or base diving off a cliff. Because risking an emotional choice does not hazard physical harm, there should be no flinching away from trusting your ability to develop more vulnerable, believable characters.

"Twenty years from now you will be more disappointed by the things that you didn't do than by the ones you did do. So, throw off the bowlines. Sail away from the safe harbor. Catch the wind in your sails. Explore. Dream. Discover."

–**Mark Twain**

ROLE PLAYING: Improvisation of assuming or adopting the qualities of another. Since the real qualities of another person are inaccessible, role-playing depends on the qualities of the person doing the role-playing.

SINGULAR: Being only one, peculiar, remarkable.

STORY: A sequence of events. A story is the formation of words and images that represent real life.

TALENT: Its root and as its definition are found in desire, inclination, will. It is also defined as a special natural ability, or gift. Your talent lies in your desire to affect an audience. It is also your drive to succeed which is as important as your quirks, emotions and point of view.

VINDICATE/VINDICATION: Clear of blame. To return like for like, to avenge. Succeeding against another's opinion of you, succeeding against your own inner critic, trusting your ideas and being rewarded for that trust is great vindication.

VULNERABLE: Susceptible to being wounded, open to attack, criticism or temptation. To be vulnerable is to be open to potential harm. Many actors hide their vulnerability or areas where they might be criticized. Yet within these areas of susceptibility lies the actor's talent. Characters that affect an audience are open, raw and sensitive. In this sense a strong character is one who overcomes or survives inspite of any vulnerability.

Hidden Acting Agendas exist to protect vulnerability. When an actor backs down from a potent ingredient, exposing his or her ability to present that ingredient, it's the vulnerability of being wrong and open to attack that motivates the flinches. Developing your acting menu, with risk, allows you exposure to being wrong and can result in the most meaningful lessons. Without vulnerability a character ceases to be truly affecting. Vulnerability leads to personal power for actors.

WHAT IF?: A question you can ask yourself that fires up your imagination. The question could be: "What if the character was me—what would I do?"

WILLING: Cheerfully ready. To me a willing actor is one who is excited about trying, exploring and developing. Willing is not an actor who goes reluctantly along .

About the Author

Bill Howey has been teaching and coaching acting for over twenty-five years, first in Los Angeles and currently in Denver.

Bill began acting professionally at The Cleveland Playhouse. During his career Bill has appeared on television and in film, on stage, produced live television, written and directed three independent movies, and directed award winning plays. He also has worked as the acting/dialogue coach for several television series.

Bill trains and consults managers, executives and public speakers, in a variety of businesses.

Bill can be contacted at billhowey@actorsmenu.com.

Comments from Bill's Acting Students:

"I have studied with Bill Howey for many years, in Los Angeles and in Denver. I have also studied with other teachers, some of the best in LA. And the impact Bill's class has on my acting stands the test of time, whereas the others do not.

The environment Bill creates is one of absolute trust, and atmosphere in which a student feels they can try anything without the fear of judgement. Bill's class lays the ground work for a very solid base from which to work and I owe my success to his expertise and intuition."

—John Scott Clough

"Bill Howey's class opens the door to emotions that we all bury to stay in our comfort zones. Bill has taught me that in order to grow as an actor you must do the things that frighten and challenge you the most.

—Amy Rome

"Bill is an incredibly inspiring teacher who challenges me in a way few teachers have done. I have over 40 stage, film/video and commercial credits, including producing and directing credits. I have previously worked with other teachers/coaches for seven years and I've been with Bill for an additional four years.

Bill is honest, sincere, trustworthy, and passionate. His candid and direct approach personalized to each individual actor's work is admirable and nothing short of amazing. He identifies each actor's unique problem(s) and encourages every one of us to produce truthful and exciting work."

—Anna Hadzi

"Viva el Howey! It was he who instructed me on being natural and charming. I've learned to let go of negative attitudes."
—Daniel Palmer 15

"In the four years I've been studying with Bill, I've developed the utmost respect for his teaching style and methods. My confidence in and my passion for acting have grown.
—Kari Young

"My acting changed after studying with Bill Howey but my life has also changed. Bill is passionate, challenging, nurturing, brilliant, insightful, encouraging, intense, and respectful. He is one who seeks our interest and desires our success.

Bill has opened up a whole new world full of emotion and made it a safe place to express those emotions. He has given me a level of confidence I never knew I possessed. He has tapped into the core of my being and is teaching me how to trust my intuitions and find the inner strength that has always been rooted there."
—Liz Randall

"Bill provides a safe workspace for actors to experiment and take risks. Bill is passionate about his work and that of his students. That passion, along with his sense of humor breeds an unparalleled level of trust between teacher and student."
—Barbara Matthews

"Bill shows a unique way of bringing out your true person and feelings into a character. He is gifted in guiding actors and opening doors in an actor's mind."
—Megan Hatfield 16

" Bill is an incredible teacher. His teen workshop was not only intense but I learned approaches to scenes I had not focused on before. "

—Jessica Archer 14

" Bill is an amazing teacher. He has a special way of communicating with people. He works one on one with each actor to bring out their best acting. Each time I come I learn something new about myself and my acting techniques. I always have so much fun that's it's a bummer when it's over."

—Amanda Smetzer 14

"It's a wonderful experience to learn from someone who exhibits the kind of fervor Bill does in his work. He has redefined what acting is and puts it into terms that not only deepens the work but inspires you in such a way that makes it a richer, more personal experience. His intentions are always aimed at helping you and getting you to be true to the work."

—Bill Hofto

"Bill has a knack for giving the kind of constructive feedback that causes light bulbs to go off in your head."

—Leigh Orr

"I had no training prior to Bill's class. While studying with Bill I found an agent and had the lead in an independent feature film. Bill loves his work, he loves what he does, and he tries to pass that on to his students. Because without passion....what is acting? The result: art imitates life, not only has my art gotten better but so has my life. I can't be thankful enough.

—Marco Cicione

Quote Citations

Adams, John Quincy—6th President of the United States.

Aristotle—philosopher.

Baldwin, James—novelist, essayist.
    Quote from *Go Tell it on the Mountain*.

Benchley, Robert—humorist, drama critic, actor.
    Quote used with permission of Nat Benchley

Coolidge, Calvin—13th President of the United States.
    Quote from his speech delivered to the Massachusetts
    Senate 1914.

Cummings, E.E.—poet, artist, playwright.
    Excerpt from *A Poet's Advice to Students*.
    Copyright © (1958, 1965) by The Trustees for the
    E.E. Cummings Trust. Copyright © (1958, 1965)
    by George J. Firmage, from *A MISCELLANY REVISED*
    by E.E. Cummings. Edited by George J. Firmage.
    Used by permission of Liverlight Publishing
    Corporation.

Diderot, Denis—French writer and philosopher.

Egri, Lajos—author, playwright.
    Quote from *The Art of Dramatic Writing* used with
    permission of Ted Egri.

Ekman, Paul, PhD.
    (2003). *Emotions Revealed*. Times Books.
    Quote used with permission of Paul Ekman.

Eliot, George (Mary Ann Evans)—novelist.

Emerson, Ralph Waldo—author, poet and philosopher.

Forster, E. M.—British writer.
Quote from *Aspects of the Novel* with permission of "The Provost and Scholars of King's College, Cambridge and The Society of Authors as the literary representatives of the Estate of E. M. Forster." Harcourt, Orlando, FL.

Foster, John W.—British clergyman, essayist.

Galileo—Astronomer and Physicist.

Gibran, Kahlil—poet, artist.

Goethe, Johann Wolfgang von (1749–1832) German writer, philosopher, humanist.

Goleman, Daniel, PhD.
(1995). *Emotional Intelligence*. Bantam Books.
Quote used with permission of Daniel Goleman.

Gombrich, E.H.—art critic, historian, writer.
Reproduced from *Art & Illusion: A Study in the Psychology of Pictorial Representation* by E.H. Gombrich, sixth edition (p.172) © 2002 Phaidon Press Limited

Graham, Martha—dancer, choreographer.
Quote from *Martha: The Life and Work of Martha Graham* by Agnes de Mille.

Hillis, Newell Dwight—author
(1912). *The Misfortune of a World Without Pain*.

Hindi Proverb.

Holmes, Oliver Wendell— author.

Horace—Roman poet (65 BC – 8 BC)

Horton, Andrew.
   (1994). *Writing the Character Centered Screenplay.*
   University of California press.
   Quote used with permission of Andrew Horton.

Jong, Erica—author, educator.
   Quote from *The Craft of Poetry.* Ed. by W. Packard.

Law, Vernon Sanders—pitcher Pittsburgh pirates.
   Quote used with permission of Vernon Sanders Law.

Nin, Anais—diarist

Seneca—philosopher.

Scott, George C.—actor.
   Quote © (1968) TIME Inc. reprinted by permission.

Shaw, George Bernard—dramatist, literary critic.

Stanislavski, Konstantin (Constantin) (1863–1938)

Twain, Mark—writer.

Van Dyke, Henry—clergyman, author, educator.

Vogler, Christopher.
   (1992). *The Writers Journey: Mythic Structure for
   Storytellers and Screenwriters.* Michael Wiese Productions.
   Quote used with permission of Christopher Vogler.

Wilde, Oscar—playwright, poet.

Index

The Actor's Menu®

A Character Preparation Handbook

 Compass Publishing

Order Form

To order copies of *The Actor's Menu* you can:

Fax this form to: 1-303-989-1883

Order via telephone 1-303-989-8654

Email orders to: <u>orders@actorsmenu.com</u>

Postal order: Compass Publishing, The Actor's Menu by Bill Howey, P.O. Box 280188, Lakewood, Colorado, 80228-0188, USA

Please send ____copies of *The Actor's Menu*. I understand that I may return the book for a full refund.

Name:_____

Address:_____

City:_____ State:_____Zip: _____

Telephone: _____

Email address:_____

Sales Tax: Please add 4.6% for books sent to Colorado addresses.

Shipping: $5.00 for first book and $2.00 for each additional book.

$14.95 for each book ordered for a total of	$_____
Shipping for first book	$ 5.00
Shipping for each additional book	$_____
Subtotal:	$_____
Sales Tax of 4.6% CO	$_____
Total:	$_____

(Books are shipped by United States Priority Mail)

Payment is by check to:

Compass Publishing
The Actor's Menu by Bill Howey
P.O. Box 280188
Lakewood, CO 80228-0188